Making Folk Toys
& Weather Vanes

Making Folk Toys
& Weather Vanes

Sharon Pierce

 Sterling Publishing Co. Inc. New York

Edited by Katherine Balch
Designed by Karen Nelson

Library of Congress Cataloging in Publication Data
Pierce, Sharon.
 Making folk toys & weather vanes.

 Bibliography: p.
 Includes index.
 1. Wooden toy making. 2. Weather vanes. I. Title.
II. Title: Making folk toys and weather vanes.
TT174.5.W6P54 1984   745.592   84-8461
ISBN 0-8069-7906-2 (pbk.)

     5   7   9   10   8   6   4

Copyright © 1984 by Sharon Pierce
Published by Sterling Publishing Co., Inc.
Two Park Avenue, New York, N.Y. 10016
Distributed in Australia by Capricorn Book Co. Pty. Ltd.
Unit 5C1 Lincoln St., Lane Cove, N.S.W. 2066
Distributed in the United Kingdom by Blandford Press
Link House, West Street, Poole, Dorset BH15 1LL, England
Distributed in Canada by Oak Tree Press Ltd.
ᶜ/o Canadian Manda Group, P.O. Box 920, Station U
Toronto, Ontario, Canada M8Z 5P9
Manufactured in the United States of America

In Memory of My Mother

Thank you to my family and friends who have always encouraged me, and especially to my husband and children who have given me room to grow.

A very special thank you to Katherine Balch, my editor, for her enthusiasm and her expertise, and to Karen Nelson for all her artistic touches, especially the cover design.

TABLE OF CONTENTS

Introduction   9
Folk Art in America   13
Folk Art Designs & Patterns   15
Wood Selection   17
Materials & Equipment   19

FOLK TOYS   23

The Rocking Horse   25
   Rocking Horse   27
Wheel Toys   33
   Reindeer on Wheels   35
   Pony on Wheels   40
   Goat on Wheels   45
Articulated Folk Toys   49
   Cocoa Bunny & Marshmallow   51
   Piggy   56
   Bitsybear, American Bear, Honeybear   59
   Mama Duck & Duckling   64
   Pan & Nandy Pandas   68
   Barney the Cat   72
   Bosco the Dog   75

WEATHER VANES   79

Weather Vanes   81
   Running Horse Weather Vane   83
   Sea Serpent Weather Vane   87
   Running Rabbit Weather Vane   91
   Goat Weather Vane   94
   Pig Weather Vane   97

Metric Conversion Chart   101
American & British Terms   103
Bibliography   105
Index   107
Photo Credit   111
About the Author   112

INTRODUCTION

*I*t has been most enjoyable combining two of my favorite activities—designing and writing—while working on this book. I find folk toys and weather vanes fascinating. These Folk Toys are appreciated by both children and adults, and the Weather Vanes add a bit of country charm to any decor.

All of the projects in this book are simple enough for beginning woodworkers. Detailed instructions have been given for each step. The Weather Vanes were designed as decorative pieces, but the patterns can be adapted for outdoor use by substituting sheet metal for the wood and by attaching the rod to the full width of the vane. The Folk Toys can be used either for play or for decoration. As with any toy, exercise good judgment when presenting certain playthings to children

younger than three. Until the child is older, the toys can be used to add a little whimsy to an empty nook.

In order to make this book as easy to follow as possible, I have repeated instructions so that readers will not have to flip from page to page. Also, I am a self-taught folk artist, so some of my techniques may sound rather unconventional, but from trial and error, I have found that these methods work best.

I consider the projects in this book to be fun. Even though they definitely require work, it is fun work. You'll see what I mean when you put the finishing touches on your first project. I hope you enjoy making these Folk Toys and Weather Vanes as much as I do.

EDITOR'S NOTE

Patterns for some of the toys and vanes are too large to reproduce in this book. They have been reduced, therefore, by 25% and printed on top of a ¾-in. grid. To enlarge these patterns so you can use the sizes of materials given in the directions, buy 1-in. grid paper or make your own. Draw a portion of the original pattern—horse's ears on page 85, for example—one square at a time. Make the line running through the 1-in. square correspond directly to the line running through the book's ¾-in. square. After enlarging the pattern in this way, cut it out and continue instructions for making the poster-board pattern.

FOLK ART IN AMERICA

Folk art is a part of the American heritage. Since the Pilgrims landed in 1620, emigrants from Europe, Africa, and Asia have brought with them centuries of cultural expression in the everyday articles of living. Cabinetmakers painted elaborate tulip designs on kitchen side boards, basket weavers improvised from old designs for New World uses, and quilters fashioned new patterns from age-old techniques. The period of greatest productivity and highest quality was from 1776 to 1876.

In colonial America, toys were made by both professional carvers and amateur whittlers, such as fathers and mothers, friends and journeymen. Children delighted in dolls and miniature houses and in blocks of wood shaped and painted to look like horses, cows, or their pet dog. Some toys were put on wheels or made with movable arms and legs.

Although treasured by generations of children, these toys and folk art in general were not considered a true art form until the 1920s. Nineteenth-century art collectors thought it crude and simplistic; the motifs were too flat, the colors primitive, and the subjects ordinary. And yet these are the very characteristics we find so appealing today, in a century that has managed to mechanize nearly every item in the home and office. Suddenly the absence of shading brings the subject closer to us, the colors appear bright and cheerful, and the subjects themselves appear amusing. The distortions, in fact, are what make folk art honest, unencumbered, and full of homespun imagination instead of scholastic technique.

Many folk art motifs are now used as focal points or accent pieces in both colonial- and contemporary-style decorating. From heart trivets to pineapple lamps, the country look has become increasingly popular. As the demand and prices for the originals increase, reproductions and new folk art are being produced in the once forgotten crafts of woodworking, iron forging, and elaborate needlework. These modern reminders of the past may well become the heirlooms of tomorrow.

This interest in America's folk art has also spawned the opening or the expansion of several museums across the country. Just a few that are devoted primarily to folk art are the Museum of American Folk Art, New York; Shelburne Museum, Shelburne, Vermont; Abby Aldrich Rockefeller Folk Art Center, Williamsburg, Virginia; and the Craft and Folk Art Museum, Los Angeles. Larger museums, like The Metropolitan Museum of Art and the Whitney Museum of American Art, both in New York, have incorporated folk art into their collections.

Sometimes called the art of the common man, folk art seems destined to continue as the artistic expression for many ordinary people. And as long as there are children, there will be toys made from simple materials on a moment's notice to please them.

FOLK ART DESIGNS & PATTERNS

Folk art designs are less an imitation and more a likeness of ordinary objects. They are designs that try not so much for realism but for resemblance. After making several of the toys outlined in this book, you may want to create your own designs. If so, you'll find that it's more fun to design a pig sitting up, eating a slice of watermelon, than to try to design an actual pig standing on all fours. And if you feel inclined to make a cow playing a violin, do it! A touch of whimsy is definitely in order here. There are no hard and fast rules when making folk art.

Many pieces of wooden folk art are of animals that are common to rural life. This does not mean, however, that modern folk art is limited to rural subjects. Since most people now live in cities, it may be the cityscape that inspires urban folk artists. And even though 50 folk artists may carve 50 cows, each will produce a different interpretation. So if your idea sounds like someone else's don't be discouraged; your interpretation and execution will certainly be unique.

Just as each piece of art is different, each individual creates art in a different manner. Some craftsmen sketch their idea and then carve, whittle, or cut out their concept. Others draw either a rough or a precise pattern and then trace it onto the wood. And still others simply pick up a piece of wood and immediately carve away the unnecessary portions. After some practice, you will quickly discover the best method.

Once you have formulated an idea, it is time to translate it into an actual design. The process of designing is really very simple. The first step is to sketch in pencil the basic outline of your concept. If you need help drawing it, consult a book or encyclopedia for sketches or photos. But remember, the goal is not to make an exact replica. In fact, the less detailed and more basic your drawing, the easier it will be to translate into wood.

The next step is to erase the lines you are not satisfied with and make the necessary corrections. Occasionally I must draw a body or head ten times before it comes out right.

Once the basic sketch is finished, draw over the design to give it a bold outline. For the Folk Toys, draw the actual outline of the legs and ears as they will appear on the finished piece (see Illus. 1). Then draw these appendages separately and cut them out. Cut out the body excluding appendages. Now you have all the pattern pieces.

Trace these pattern pieces onto a heavy paper, such as poster board, and cut them out. You now have a template that can be used many times. Place this posterboard pattern on the wood, making sure it runs lengthwise with the grain (Illus. 22).

I always enjoy making the first piece from a pattern, even though I may eventually alter some details. Often the original piece is the worst, but it improves with slight modifications. This, of course, means making a completely new pattern so that all the pieces fit. On the other hand, I am occasionally pleased with my first finished piece. It's a matter of trial and error.

a.   b.   c.

Illus. 1. Making your own pattern: (a) draw complete figure; (b) trace forelegs, hind legs, ears, etc., separately and cut out; (c) cut out body, excluding appendages.

WOOD SELECTION

Wood. It sounds rather plain and uninteresting, doesn't it? Yet many species have exotic names, such as madrone, padauk, tanguile, and claro, with colors just as unusual. Carvers, over the years, have used whatever wood was at hand, whether it was Indonesian jelutong or Vermont maple.

After working with other materials, I have finally decided to work primarily with wood. I like what you can do with the wood, the possibilities, the smell of the wood, the feel of the wood. I am most familiar with the softwoods and have used them for most of the projects.

Softwood comes from coniferous trees. I have used either pine or spruce, bought in boards measuring 1 x 10 or 1 x 12, indicating 1 in. thick by 10 or 12 in. wide. However, the thickness is actually ¾ in. after mill planing. Any length may be purchased.

A portion of the softwood that I buy is then planed to a ⅜-in. thickness. This is needed for the legs and arms of all the Folk Toys and also for the Weather Vanes made of softwood rather than ¼-in. birch plywood. Some lumberyards will plane the wood to ⅜-in. or any desired thickness; others will not. Be sure to ask first.

Consider the following when buying wood:

Pine. Choose a white pine if possible. Yellow pine, because of its higher resin content, is harder to cut. The No. 2 sugar pine is a good choice. It is soft, white, and has medium-size knots. The knots are small enough to work around.

Also available is clear white, more expensive pine with no knots. Pine shelving is acceptable if you can find pieces that are not warped and that are not a yellow pine.

Spruce. Choose a white spruce, which usually has smaller knots. This wood is only slightly harder than the pine, and both are excellent to work with. Cutting of either is about the same. The spruce, however, takes a little more sanding.

Kiln dried. Most woods today are kiln

dried, but it is advisable to check as green wood will most certainly warp.

Cupping and Splitting. When choosing wood, check for two culprits: cupping and splitting. Cupping is the curved shape a piece of lumber can take and is noticeable at the board's ends. If they are not perfectly straight, they are cupped, or bowed. And as you can imagine, a curved piece of wood will produce numerous problems. If areas in the lumber have separated, apply a little pressure above and below these splits to determine their extent. I usually avoid using boards with splits unless they are at the ends of the board only.

Birch plywood. Use birch plywood for the Weather Vanes and for the ears, hearts, horns, and legs of the Folk Toys. It has a nice, birch veneer on both sides and is solid throughout without the "holes" that are characteristic of regular plywood. Rarely have I encountered holes in birch plywood. It is extremely easy to cut and sands well.

MATERIALS & EQUIPMENT

Know your materials and equipment well. Following is a list of both with tips to make work easier and time more productive.

Materials

WOOD

The two types of wood needed are softwood, ¾ in. and ⅜ in. thick and birch plywood, ¼ in. thick. See pp. 17–18 for details.

WOODEN DOWELS

The size needed for the Articulated Folk Toys is ⅛ in. This is a critical selection as these dowels are not perfect in diameter or uniform in roundness. The thinnest dowels, which I use, take a 7/64-in. drill bit. If the dowels are thicker, use a ⅛-in. drill bit. Be sure to drill sample holes in scrap wood to see which fits. The dowel should tap into the hole easily, but not pull out easily. If the fit is too tight, the dowel will eventually break when the arm or leg is moved. For extra durability for the jointed toys, try using the next larger dowel and bit size.

For the Folk Toys' wheels, use dowels 1 in. in diameter. These are cut uniformly with the band saw.

2 x 4 LUMBER

Any weather-beaten or new piece of 2 x 4 will do, as it is used only for the base of the Weather Vane and can be left weathered looking or stained.

METAL RODS

These are used for the Weather Vanes and should be 3/32 in. in diameter. If unavailable, use a metal clothes hanger. Make sure the rod is straight. Cut to appropriate length with cutters and be sure to sand or file edges so they are not sharp.

SANDPAPER

I use only medium and fine grades of sandpaper for softwoods. Always sand with the grain of the wood, using medium paper first and finishing with fine. Use medium-grade sandpaper for both stationary belt sander and sanding wheel.

PAINT

All projects have been painted with acrylic tube paints, which are water-soluble but permanent once dry. Before starting to paint, always dip the brush into water first, and then blot dry. Paint light areas first, remembering to paint the edges before the flat surfaces. Paint with the grain of the wood, smoothing out brush strokes as you paint. Also, remember that the color of the paint will darken when dry. All amounts are approximations and should be adjusted if necessary to achieve the right tone.

STAIN

The Wheel Toys and Rocking Horse are stained instead of painted. Stain types and colors vary widely. Choose one that is easy to apply and appropriate to the piece. When I want an older look, I use a stain with sealer in it, which eliminates applying one later. At other times, I use a regular stain and then apply a semigloss spray sealer for a more finished look. A word of caution, however, is always try the stain and sealer on a scrap piece to ensure compatibility. Some sealers will lift certain stains. Shellac, of course, should not be used for toys that children might put in their mouth because it is water soluble. Polyurethane, however, is safe.

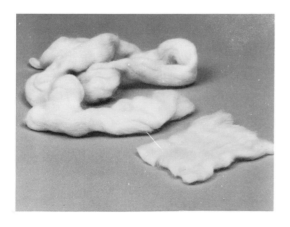

BRUSHES

Use small, firm brushes. I use ½-in.-flat and ¾-in.-bright brushes. Painting the eyes requires a ¹⁄₁₆-in. brush. Buy quality brushes from an art supply store; the higher price will be justified by the durability of the better brush. Be sure to wash out the brush immediately after each use.

WOOD GLUE

Any white or yellow glue made specifically for wood is suitable, as long as it dries clear. Be especially careful not to get glue onto any area of the wood that will be stained, as the stain will not take properly where glue has been. If the glue does smear, however, sand the area well with the grain of the wood to remove most of the glue.

Miscellaneous items needed for some projects are:

Acrylic fibre. Called roving, this material is used for the mane of the Rocking Horse and tails of the Wheel Toys (Illus. 2). Buy it at a weaver's shop or at an arts and crafts shop. One brand is called Feel O' Fleece by Plaid Enterprises. Another is a natural-colored craft fur that most craft shops sell. Toys made with this acrylic fibre should, of course, not be given to toddlers who might think it's edible.

Brass escutcheon pins (⅝-in.). This is a fancy name for a brass tack with a rounded head. These are used to attach the wheels to the Wheel Toys.

Illus. 2. Acrylic fibre (roving)

Screw eyes. These small screws are screwed into the bases of the Wheel Toys to hold the string.

Ribbon, string, felt. These are for the finishing touches.

Tracing paper. This transparent paper is good for tracing patterns from the book.

Poster board (thin cardboard). Make pattern templates that can be re-used from this thin cardboard.

Equipment

GOGGLES

Always wear some type of eye protection, such as goggles or glasses, when cutting, sanding, or drilling. Goggles that fit snugly over the eyes are best.

DUST MASK

These masks prevent hazardous dust particles from entering the lungs. They are recommended if you do much woodworking and are required for some woods, like mahogany.

TABLETOP SCROLL SAW

This saw is safe enough to be used by children. It has a replaceable, vibrating blade and is especially useful for small intricate work, such as the ears and hearts cut out of ¼-in. birch plywood. It also cuts the softwoods well, but takes a little longer than the band saw. Choose a fine-tooth blade suitable for intricate cutting. My scroll saw has a shaft for a sanding wheel, which eliminates most hand sanding. Always remove the sanding wheel when not in use.

BAND SAW

A small band saw for hobby-type purposes works well for these projects. The thin, continuous blade should be ⅛ in. wide with at least 15 teeth per inch. The band saw is easy to use but cannot make intricate cuts as easily as the scroll saw. Be sure therefore to make relief cuts (Illus. 3) when approaching a sharp curve or an angle.

SANDER

There are three choices for sanding here: the sanding wheel on the scroll saw (Illus. 4), a small stationary belt sander,

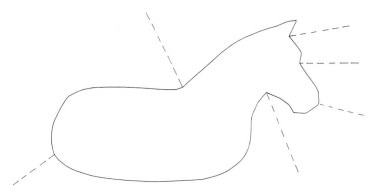

Illus. 3. Relief cuts: dotted lines represent cuts that should be made prior to cutting out shape with the band saw.

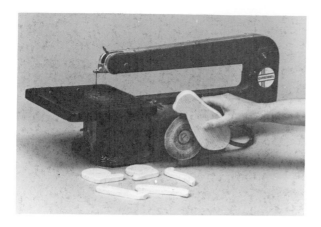

Illus. 4. Scroll saw with sanding wheel

or sandpaper and good old arm power. Whichever method you choose, remember when sanding the Folk Toys to hold the edge at an angle to the sandpaper to achieve a carved effect. This is one of the most important steps. Final sanding is done by hand with fine sandpaper, as is the sanding of the birch plywood.

DRILL
Any portable hand drill is suitable for the small amount of drilling needed for each project.

DRILL STAND (not a drill press)
This is a rather inexpensive way to ensure straight drilling and is a great help to me. If the holes are not drilled straight, the toys will not stand level. This is an optional piece of equipment.

HAMMER
A small tack hammer is sufficient.

NIPPERS/CUTTERS
Wood nippers are needed to cut the wooden dowels for the Articulated Folk Toys; metal cutters are needed for the Weather Vane rods.

Folk Toys

THE ROCKING HORSE

*B*efore the invention of the automobile, the horse symbolized adventure, independence, and romance to children from China to Colorado. For nearly three centuries children have ridden hobbyhorses—a stick with the head of a horse at one end and wheels on the other. Then came the carved horse, standing on a platform or cart and placed on wheels. And finally, the rocking horse was invented.

The first British rocking horses appeared in the 17th century and for the most part were rather crudely shaped. But gradually the details and shape became more realistic. In 1785 William Long, an American cabinetmaker originally from London, advertised in the *Pennsylvania Packet* his rocking horses as a way to teach children to ride and to provide them exercise. By the end of the 18th century the rocking horse as we know it today—with a lifelike, carved body set on graceful, curved rockers—had evolved. This playful reminder of bygone days is still appealing both as a toy and as a decorative piece.

Rocking Horse

MATERIALS

Softwood, ¾ in. thick: one piece
10 x 18 in.
Softwood, ⅜ in. thick: one piece
7 x 10 in.
Stain: light walnut and dark walnut
Natural-colored acrylic fibre (roving)
Felt (optional): gold, 3 x 5 in.; brown,
2 x 4 in.
Sandpaper: medium and fine grades
Wood glue
Finishing nails: 1¼ in. long, four
Flathead wood screws: ¾ x 4, four

TOOLS

Scroll saw or band saw
Drill with 3/16-in. and ⅛-in. bits
Stationary belt sander or sanding wheel
(optional): with medium-grade sandpaper
Scissors
C-clamps

INSTRUCTIONS

Pattern. Trace pattern pieces onto paper
and cut out. Then trace around pattern
onto heavy paper or poster board and cut
out. Lay poster-board patterns for horse's
body and rockers onto ¾-in.-thick softwood. It is extremely important that the
length of the pattern pieces runs with the

Illus. 5.

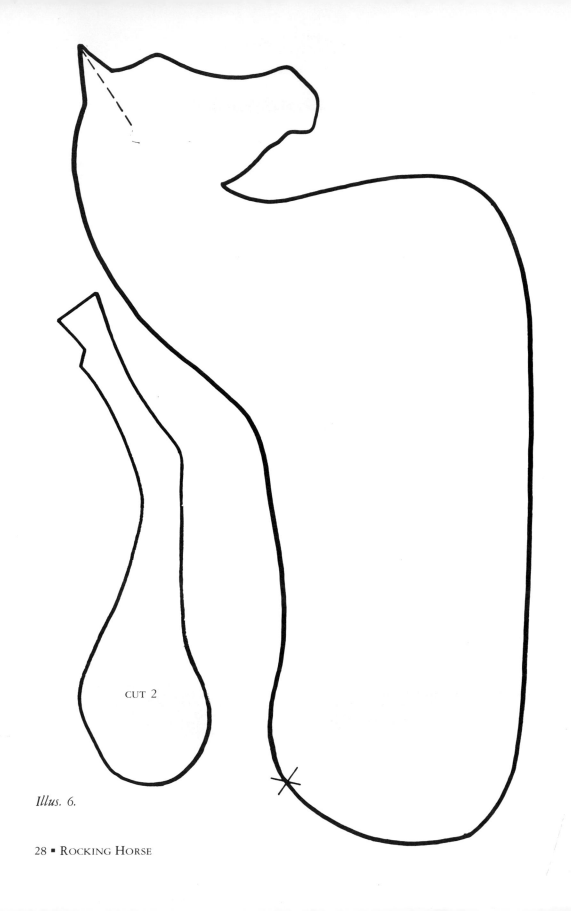

CUT 2

Illus. 6.

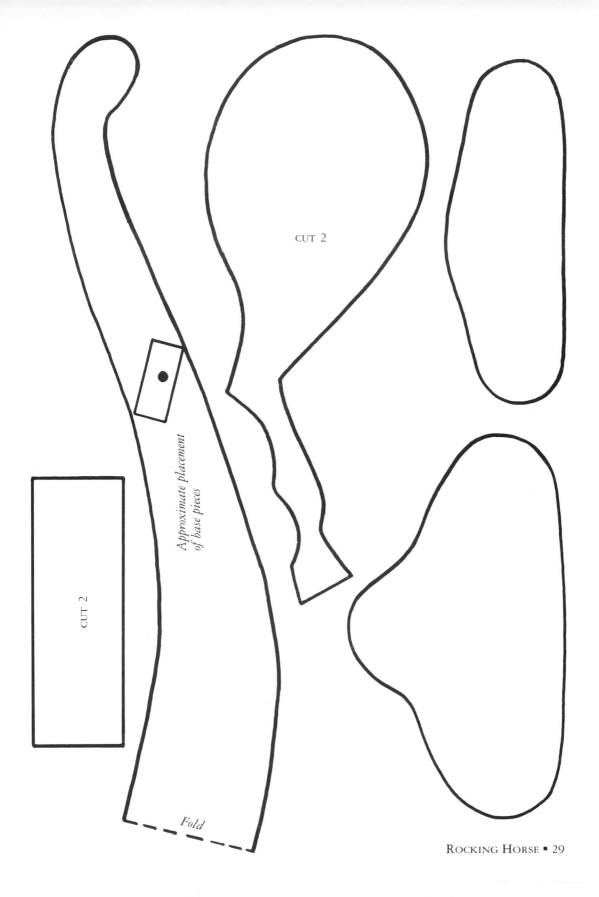

CUT 2

CUT 2

Approximate placement of base pieces

Fold

ROCKING HORSE ▪ 29

grain of the wood (see Illus. 22, for example) to ensure strength of the cut pieces. Trace patterns onto wood.

Next, trace the poster-board patterns for two forelegs, two hind legs, and two base pieces onto the ⅜-in.-thick softwood.

Cutting. With scroll or band saw, cut out all pieces. Cut slowly and accurately. To form two ears cut out and discard a small **V**-shaped section from top of head (Illus. 8).

Drilling. Using the ³⁄₁₆-in. bit, drill a hole where marked in Illus. 6 to hold the horse's tail.

Sanding. As mentioned before, this is a critical step. Starting with the body, move the edges against the sander at an angle to produce a rounded, carved effect. Hold the body at slightly different angles to get a rounder edge (Illus. 4). If sanding by hand use medium-grade sandpaper.

Sand the legs in the same manner, but sand the inside (which will be glued to the body) only lightly and retain relatively square edges; sand outside edge rounded. Be sure to sand a right and left leg, front and back. Sand the rockers to produce rounded edges. Sand the bases only lightly by hand and retain relatively square edges. Give each piece a final sanding by hand with fine-grade sandpaper, going with the grain.

Assembling horse. First, lay right foreleg

and right hind leg in proper position for gluing (see Illus. 7). To ensure that the horse will stand evenly on all fours, place hooves of right legs up against a perfectly level and squared scrap of wood about 12 in. long (see Illus. 15). Then set the body on the legs. Place a small scrap of ⅜-in.-thick wood underneath the horse's head to keep the body level. Now, to check accuracy of gluing position, place the left legs on body with hooves flush against the 12-in. wood. Make light pencil marks on body to indicate position. Remove left legs. Make light pencil marks on right legs. Set body aside.

Place about three drops of glue in the middle of each right leg where it will attach to the body. Smooth this out with a finger, being very careful not to push it near the edges, where it might smear and prevent that area from taking the stain. Now, carefully set the horse's body on top of the right legs. Glue left legs and put them on body. Be sure the hooves are still flat against the 12-in.-long scrap of wood. Place a flat piece of wood across the upper part of the legs (glued area) and weight it with something fairly heavy. Let dry.

Staining. Wearing rubber gloves, dip a cloth into the light walnut stain (all brands are different shades, so you may want a different color), spreading it over the entire horse and then wiping off the excess.

Stain rockers and base a dark walnut or a

shade darker than the stain used on the horse. Let dry.

Note: If using a stain with no sealer, apply a polyurethane or lacquer finish. Just buff it to a slight sheen when it is perfectly dry.

Final assembling. Place two thin scraps of wood, about 2 in. wide and 12 in. long, 2 in. apart and stand them on edge. Place bases on top of these scraps about 8 in. apart. Now, place rockers up against bases (see Illus. 6 for approximate base position). Set the horse on top of the bases, making sure hooves are centered; mark bases lightly with pencil where hooves and rockers meet bases. Adjust position as necessary.

Remove horse and glue bases to rockers.

Place one thin scrap of wood on the outside of each rocker where bases join rockers. Position C-clamps over scraps and carefully screw into place. Let dry at least 30 minutes. Drill holes through rockers and into bases. Tap in finishing nails.

Re-position horse on bases where marked in pencil. Glue hooves into place, centering them on the bases. For added strength, when glue is absolutely dry, use ⅛-in. bit and drill holes 1¼ in. deep up through base and into center of each hoof. Hold the leg you are drilling with your free hand to feel if the drill bit starts

Illus. 7. Gluing position for Rocking Horse

to exit through the side of the horse's leg (Illus. 47); insert screws.

Mane. Cut a strip of acrylic fibre (roving) 5½ in. long. Also cut a piece ¾ in. to 1 in. long for the forelock. Twist one end of the forelock and glue it into place between the ears. Put glue only between the ears so the hair hangs freely on the forehead.

Next, take the piece for the mane and spread the fibres out to about 4 in. wide, keeping the length at 5½ in. It will be flatter now, like a blanket. Spread a thin layer of glue on the top of the horse from the ears to the curve where the back meets the neck. Carefully place the center of the roving along the glue and lightly pat this into place. Do not let the glue soak through completely. Let this dry for about 15 minutes.

Take a needle or pin and gently comb through the mane (unglued side sections). Do not be concerned about the few pieces that pull through. After the mane is well shaped, take a small scissors and trim the bottom edge at an angle (see Illus. 5). To keep the mane in place, lift it just enough to squeeze a thin line or two of glue underneath and lightly pat it down.

Tail. Cut a 3½-in. strip of roving. Twist one end, apply a little glue, and twist again. Let dry for about five minutes. Put a few drops of glue into hole drilled for the tail. Now, take a thin, pointed object and push the twisted end of the tail into the hole. Groom the tail, like the mane, with a pin and scissors.

Saddle (optional). Trace patterns for the saddle. Pin the smaller pattern onto dark brown felt, the larger pattern onto gold felt. Cut out. Place a drop of glue on each side of brown piece and glue to gold piece. Position saddle on horse and place a drop or two of glue under each side to hold the saddle in place.

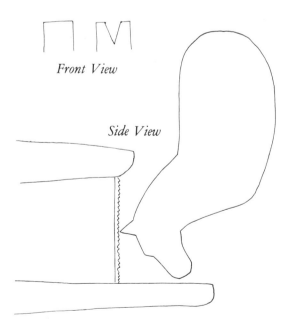

Front View

Side View

Illus. 8. Cutting ears. Side view: holding the toy vertical to the table of the saw, cut out V-shaped section for two ears. This method also applies to the Reindeer, Goat, and Pony. Front view: before and after cutting ears.

WHEEL TOYS

*C*hildren have played with these simple, yet clever, toys for centuries. Model carts with solid wheels were made as long ago as 3000 B.C. by the Sumerians who lived in the valley of the Euphrates River. Celtic and Aegean toy chariots were painted to imitate wicker, and Egyptian chariots were made of leather. A pig and a lion, both toys carved from limestone and placed on wheels to be pulled, have been found in an 1100 B.C. Persian temple. And carved into a Roman ivory chariot, 1½ in. high, are the names of winners of a real chariot race.

The hobbyhorse—a stick with a horse's head on one end and wheels on the other—which has delighted children since Socrates, was one of the earliest wooden pull toys of 18th-century America. And in the 19th century, William Schimmel popularized groups of individual animals on wheels. Two of these tableaux, the Garden of Eden and Noah's Ark, were purchased as "Sunday toys" for children who were forbidden more boisterous play on the Sabbath.

Reindeer on Wheels

MATERIALS

Softwood, ¾ in. thick: one piece 4 x 6 in.
Softwood, ⅜ in. thick: one piece 6 x 8 in.
Birch plywood, ¼ in. thick: one piece
2 x 4 in.
Wooden wheels, four, or wooden dowel
8 in. long to make wheels: 1 in. diameter
Brass escutcheon pins (round-head tacks):
⅝ in. long, four
Flathead wood screws: ¾ x 4, four
Screw eye: ½-in. long, one
Natural-colored acrylic fibre (roving), or
substitute unwoven cotton
Red ribbon: ¼ in. wide, 10 in. long
String: 3 ft. long
Acrylic paint: permanent green deep,
naphthol red light, black, white, and
burnt umber
Stain: light walnut
Brushes: ½ in. flat and 1/16 in. round
Sandpaper: medium and fine grades
Wood glue

TOOLS

Scroll saw or band saw
Drill with 1/16-in. and ⅛-in. bits
Small hammer
Stationary belt sander or sanding wheel
(optional): with medium-grade sandpaper

Illus. 9.

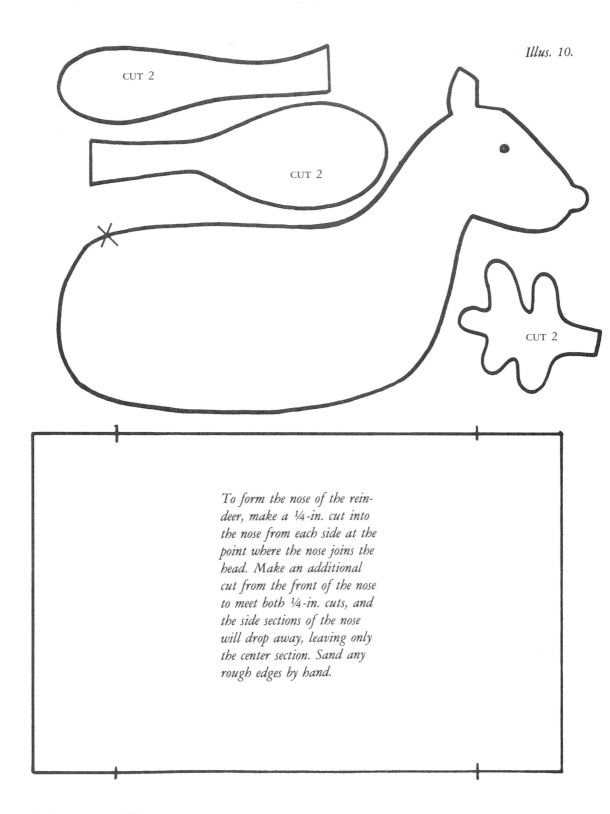

Illus. 10.

CUT 2

CUT 2

CUT 2

To form the nose of the reindeer, make a ¼-in. cut into
the nose from each side at the
point where the nose joins the
head. Make an additional
cut from the front of the nose
to meet both ¼-in. cuts, and
the side sections of the nose
will drop away, leaving only
the center section. Sand any
rough edges by hand.

INSTRUCTIONS

Pattern. Trace pattern pieces onto paper and cut out. Then trace around pattern onto heavy paper or poster board and cut out. Lay poster-board pattern of reindeer body onto ¾-in. wood and trace, ensuring that the pattern runs lengthwise with the grain of the wood (Illus. 22). Trace patterns for base, two forelegs, and two hind legs onto ⅜-in. softwood. Trace pattern for antlers onto ¼-in. wood.

Cutting. With scroll or band saw, cut out all pieces, being particularly careful when cutting the antlers. Cut a **V** into the area where the ear is to form two ears (Illus. 8).

If you have not purchased wheels, cut four discs from wooden dowel, ¼ in. thick. If your saw has a guide, use it to ensure uniform size (see Illus. 11). If not, clamp a piece of wood to the saw, running parallel to the blade, and use it as a guide to run the dowel against when cutting.

Drilling. Mark the center of each wheel and drill a hole with the ¹⁄₁₆-in. bit.

Sanding. Starting with the body, move the edges against the sander at right angles (Illus. 4) or sand by hand to produce a rounded look. Sand the base and inside edges of legs lightly retaining square edges. Sand outside edges of legs rounded. If sanding by hand, use a medium-grade paper. Give a final sanding by hand to each piece, including wheels and antlers, with fine sandpaper.

Assembling reindeer. First, lay down right foreleg and right hind leg in proper position for gluing (see Illus. 12). To ensure that the reindeer will stand evenly on all four legs, place hooves of right legs up against a perfectly level and squared scrap of wood about 3 x 8 in. (see Illus. 15). Lay body on top of the legs and put a small scrap of wood ⅜-in. thick under the head. Now position the left legs on the body with hooves resting flat against the scrap of wood. Make light pencil marks to

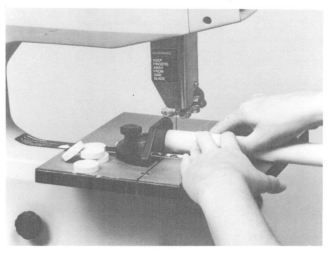

Illus. 11. Cutting wheels: from the wooden dowel, cut wheels ¼ in. thick.

indicate position. Remove left legs and body.

Place about three drops of glue on inside of each right leg where it will join the body. Smooth it out with your finger, being very careful not to spread it near the edges, where it would smear and prevent that area from taking the stain. Carefully set the reindeer body on top of the right legs. Glue left legs to body. Be sure all four hooves are resting flat. Place a flat piece of wood about 6 in. long across the upper part of the legs (glued area) and weight it down with something heavy. Let dry.

Staining. Wearing rubber gloves, stain reindeer and antlers with a cloth, wiping off the excess. If using a stain with no sealer, apply a sealer when the stain is dry. A good spray sealer is Deft; try it, or a sealer like it, on a stained sample first to see if the stain runs.

Painting. Mix a tiny drop or two of black acrylic paint with ¼ tsp. of permanent green deep. This makes a deeper green. Paint the base.

Next, mix a tiny drop of burnt umber with ¼ tsp. of naphthol red light to make a rusty red color. Paint the wheels and nose.

Antlers. Squeeze a few drops of glue onto the reindeer's forehead, just in front of and onto each ear. Put a thin layer of glue on the antlers where they will be attached. Let glue set a few minutes and

then attach antlers one at a time. Carefully hold antlers in place for a minute or so. If one keeps falling off, prop it up with a tall object next to the reindeer. Let dry.

Assembling base. Using the brass pins, hammer the wheels into the base at the points indicated on the pattern. Glue reindeer to base, centering the legs, and let dry 30 minutes. Turn upside down and with ⅛-in. bit drill holes through base and into each foot; insert flathead screws. Insert screw eye into the middle of base front.

Tail. Cut a thin strip of roving, approximately 1¼ in. long. Twist one of the ends, apply a drop of glue, and twist again. Let dry a few minutes. Place a thin layer of glue, about ½ in. square, where the tail belongs. Fold under twisted end

Illus. 12. Gluing position for Reindeer on Wheels

and position on top of glue. Pat gently in place; tail should be fluffy. When dry, trim tail with scissors so that it forms a gentle **V** shape.

Eyes. Paint a small white dot for each eye. When dry, paint a smaller dot of black inside the white dot and towards the nose.

Ribbon. Cut a 10-in. piece of red ribbon. Tie a bow around the reindeer's neck.

String. Cut a 3-ft. piece of string. Insert one end into screw eye and secure with a knot. Make a knot at the other end for easy pulling.

Pony on Wheels

MATERIALS

Softwood, ¾ in. thick: one piece
4½ x 6½ in.
Softwood, ⅜ in. thick: one piece 8 x 8 in.
Wooden wheels, four, or wooden dowel
8 in. long to make wheels: 1 in. diameter
Brass escutcheon pins (roundhead tacks):
⅝ in. long, four
Flathead wood screws: ¾ x 4, four
Screw eye: ½ in. long, one
Natural-color acrylic fibre (roving), or
substitute unwoven cotton
String: 3 ft. long
Acrylic paint: permanent green deep,
naphthol red light, burnt umber, black,
and white
Stain: light walnut
Brushes: ½ in. flat and ¹⁄₁₆ in. round
Sandpaper: medium and fine grades
Wood glue

TOOLS

Scroll saw or band saw
Drill with ¹⁄₁₆-in. and ⅛-in. bits
Small hammer
Stationary belt sander or sanding wheel
(optional): with medium-grade sandpaper
Scissors

INSTRUCTIONS

Pattern. Trace pattern pieces onto paper

Illus. 13.

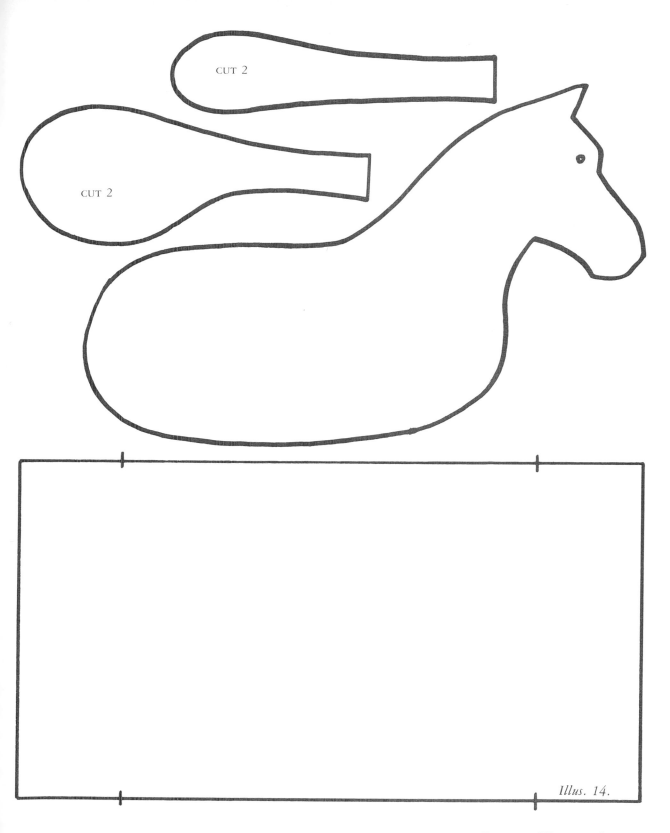

CUT 2

CUT 2

Illus. 14.

and cut out. Then trace around pattern onto heavy paper or poster board and cut out. Lay poster-board pattern of pony body onto ¾-in. wood and trace, ensuring that the pattern runs lengthwise with the grain of the wood (Illus. 22). Trace patterns for two forelegs, two hind legs, and base onto ⅜-in. softwood.

Cutting. With scroll or band saw, carefully cut out all pieces. To form two ears cut out and discard a small **V**-shaped section from top of head (Illus. 8). If you have not purchased wheels, cut four discs from wooden dowel, ¼ in. thick. If your saw has a guide, use it to ensure uniform size. If not, clamp a piece of wood to the saw, running parallel to the blade, and use it as a guide to run the dowel against when cutting.

Drilling. Mark the center of each wheel and drill a hole with the ¹⁄₁₆-in. bit.

Sanding. Starting with the body, either move the edges against the sander or sand by hand at right angles to produce a rounded look (Illus. 4). Sand base and inside edges of the legs only lightly with the sander, retaining square edges. Sand outside edges of legs rounded. Give a final sanding by hand to each piece with fine sandpaper. Sand the wheels by hand.

Assembling pony. First, place the right foreleg and right hind leg in position for gluing (see Illus. 16). To ensure that the pony will stand evenly on all four legs, place hooves of right legs up against a perfectly level and squared scrap of wood about 3 x 8 in. (see Illus. 15). Lay body on top of the legs and place a scrap of wood ⅜ in. thick under pony's head. Position the left legs on the body with hooves resting flat against scrap of wood. Make light pencil marks to indicate position. Set aside left legs and body.

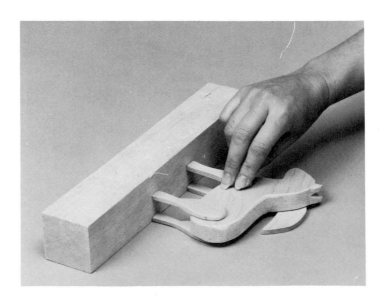

Illus. 15. Assembling the Wheel Toys: before gluing, place hooves up against a perfectly level and squared scrap of wood to ensure a level-standing toy.

Place about three drops of glue on each right leg where it will join the body. Smooth it out, being very careful not to spread it near the edges where it would smear and prevent the stain from being absorbed. Carefully put the pony body on top of the right legs. Glue left legs to body. Be sure all four hooves are resting flat. Place a flat piece of wood approximately 6 in. long across the upper part of the legs (glued area) and weight it down with something fairly heavy. Let dry.

Staining. Wearing rubber gloves, stain the pony with a cloth, wiping off any excess. If using a stain with no sealer, apply some type of sealer when the stain is dry. One good spray sealer is Deft; try it, or one like it, on a stained sample first to see if the stain runs.

Painting. Mix a tiny drop or two of black with ½ tsp. of permanent green deep to create a deeper green. Paint the base.

Next, mix a tiny drop of burnt umber with ¼ tsp. of naphthol red light to make a rusty red color. Paint the wheels.

Assembling base. Using the brass pins, hammer the wheels into the base at the points indicated on the pattern. Glue pony to base, centering the hooves, and let dry 30 minutes. Turn upside down and with ⅛-in. bit drill holes through base and into each hoof; insert flathead screws.

Insert screw eye into middle of base front.

Mane. Cut a strip of acrylic fibre (roving) about 4½ in. long for the mane. Also, cut a ¾-in. piece for the forelock. Twist one end of the forelock and glue into place between the ears. It should hang freely from the forehead.

Next, take the piece for the mane and spread the fibres out to about 3½ in. wide, keeping the length at 4½ in. Spread a thin layer of glue on top of the pony from between the ears to the curve in the back. Carefully place the center of the roving along the glue and lightly pat it in place with your fingers. Do not let the glue completely soak through the roving. Let dry for 15 minutes.

Take a needle or pin and gently comb through the mane (unglued side sections). Do not be concerned about the

Illus. 16. Gluing position for Pony on Wheels

few pieces that pull through. When the mane is well shaped, take a small pair of scissors and trim the bottom edge at an angle (Illus. 13). To keep the mane in place, lift the side sections slightly, squeeze a thin line or two of glue underneath and lightly pat into place.

Tail. Cut a strip of roving about 2½ in. long and not too thick. Twist one of the ends, put a drop of glue on it, and twist again. Let dry for five minutes. Put a ½-in. square of glue where the tail will go, then fold the twisted end under and hold in place for a minute or two.

Eyes. Paint a small dot of white for each eye. When dry, paint a smaller dot of black inside the white dot and towards the nose.

String. Cut a 3-ft. piece of string. Insert one end into screw eye and secure with a knot. Make a knot at the other end for easy pulling.

Goat on Wheels

MATERIALS

Softwood, ¾ in. thick, one piece 4 x 6 in.
Softwood, ⅜ in. thick, one piece 6 x 8 in.
Birch plywood, ¼ in. thick, one piece
1 x 2 in.
Wooden wheels, four, or wooden dowel
8 in. long to make wheels, 1 in. diameter
Brass escutcheon pins (roundhead tacks):
⅝ in. long, four

Flathead wood screws: ¾ x 4, four
Screw eye: ½ in. long, one
Natural-colored acrylic fibre (roving), or
substitute unwoven cotton
Natural-colored string, 4 ft. long
Acrylic paint: permanent green deep,
black, and white
Barnwood gray stain
Brushes: ½ in. flat and ¹⁄₁₆ in. round
Sandpaper: medium and fine grades
Wood glue

Illus. 17.

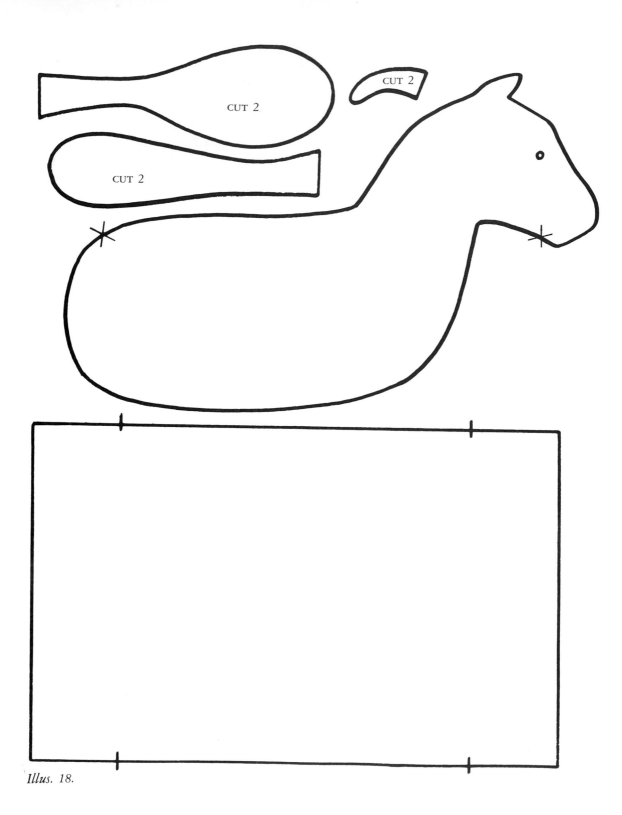

CUT 2

CUT 2

CUT 2

Illus. 18.

TOOLS

Scroll saw or band saw
Drill with 1/16-in. and 1/8-in. bits
Small hammer
Stationary belt sander or sanding wheel
(optional): with medium-grade sandpaper
Scissors

INSTRUCTIONS

Pattern. Trace pattern pieces onto paper
and cut out. Then trace around pattern
onto heavy paper or poster board. Cut
out. Lay poster-board pattern of goat body
onto 3/4-in. wood and trace, ensuring that
the pattern runs lengthwise with the
grain of the wood (Illus. 22). Trace patterns for legs and base onto 3/8-in. softwood. Trace pattern for horns onto 1/4-in.
wood.

Cutting. With the scroll or band saw,
cut out all the pieces. If possible, use a
scroll saw to cut out the horns, since they
are so small, and your fingers will be close
to the blade. To form two ears cut out
and discard a small **V**-shaped section from
top of head (Illus. 8).

If you have not purchased wheels, cut
four discs from wooden dowel, 1/4 in.
thick. If your saw has a guide, use it to
ensure uniform size. If not, clamp a piece
of wood to the saw, running parallel to
the blade, and use it as a guide to run the
dowel against when cutting.

Drilling. Mark the center of each wheel
and drill a hole with the 1/16-in. bit.

Sanding. Starting with the body, either
move the edges against the sander or sand
by hand at right angles to produce a
rounded look (Illus. 4). Sand base and inside edges of the legs only lightly, retaining square edges. Sand outside edges of
legs rounded. Give a final sanding by
hand to each piece, including horns and
wheels, with fine sandpaper.

Assembling goat. First, lay down right
foreleg and right hind leg in proper position for gluing (see Illus. 19). To ensure
that the goat will stand evenly on all four
legs, place hooves of right legs up against
a perfectly level and squared scrap of
wood about 3 x 8 in. (Illus. 15). Lay the
body on top of the legs and place a 3/8-in.
scrap of wood under goat's head.

Illus. 19. Gluing position for Goat on Wheels

Now position the left legs on the body with hooves resting flat against scrap of wood. Make light pencil marks to indicate position. Set aside left legs and body.

Place about three drops of glue on each right leg where it will join the body. Smooth it out with your finger, being very careful not to spread it near the edges, where it might smear and prevent stain from being absorbed. Carefully set the goat body on top of the right legs. Then glue left legs to body. Be sure all four hooves are resting flat. Place a flat piece of wood about 6 in. long across the upper part of the legs (glued area) and weight this down with something fairly heavy. Let dry.

Staining. Wearing rubber gloves, use a cloth to stain goat and horns, wiping off the excess. If using a stain with no sealer, apply some type of sealer when the stain is dry. Always check for compatability of stain and sealer on a small piece before using on the finished toy.

Painting. Mix a tiny drop or two of black with ½ tsp. of permanent green deep. This mixes to a deeper green. Paint the base this color.

Assembling base. Using the brass pins, hammer the wheels into the base at the points indicated on the pattern. Glue goat to base, centering legs, and let dry 30 minutes. Turn upside down and with ⅛-in. bit drill holes through base and into each foot; insert flathead screws.

Then insert screw eye into middle of base front.

Tail and beard. Cut two strips of acrylic fibre (roving) approximately 1¼ in. long. Twist one end of each, put a few drops of glue on twisted ends, and twist again. Let dry five minutes. Place a thin layer of glue, about ½ in. square, where indicated for the tail and the beard. For the tail, fold under the twisted end and position on top of glue. Pat gently into place. Make sure tail remains fluffy.

For beard, keep the twisted end back towards the neck and pat firmly into place. Both may be trimmed with scissors to form a gentle **V** shape.

Horns. Place a drop of glue on the goat's forehead and on front of ears, and also on the bottom of each horn. Place horns on forehead and hold in position for a few seconds. Let dry.

Eyes. Paint a small dot of white for each eye. When dry, paint a smaller dot of black inside the white dot and towards the nose.

String. Cut an 8-in. piece of string and tie a knot in each end. Then tie around the goat's neck.

Cut a 3-ft. piece of string. Insert one end into screw eye and secure with a knot. Make a knot at the other end for easy pulling.

ARTICULATED FOLK TOYS

My designs for toys in this chapter were inspired by early American folk toys from New England and Pennsylvania. Many of the toymakers were influenced by their German-speaking ancestors who were well known for their creativity. One such German, Albert Schoenhut, came to the United States in the middle of the 19th century and in 1903 introduced his Humpty Dumpty circus. The animals could be positioned in several ways because their arms, legs, and ears were carved separately and then joined to the body so they could move. They became the most popular toys of the time and are avidly collected today.

Cocoa Bunny & Marshmallow

MATERIALS
Cocoa Bunny
Softwood, ¾ in. thick: one piece 3 x 6 in.
Softwood, ⅜ in. thick: one piece 4 x 6 in.
Birch plywood, ¼ in. thick: one piece
2 x 3 in.
Wooden dowel: ⅛ in. diameter,
6 in. long
Acrylic paint: titanium white, burnt
umber, black
Sandpaper: medium and fine grades
Brushes: ¾ in. bright and 1⁄16 in. round

Marshmallow
Softwood, ¾ in. thick: one piece 4 x 8 in.
Softwood, ⅜ in. thick: one piece 5 x 7 in.
Birch plywood, ¼ in. thick: one piece
2½ x 3½ in.
Wooden dowel: ⅛ in. diameter, 6 in.
long
Acrylic paint: titanium white, burnt
umber, black
Sandpaper: medium and fine grades
Brushes: ¾ in. bright and 1⁄16 in. round

Illus. 20.

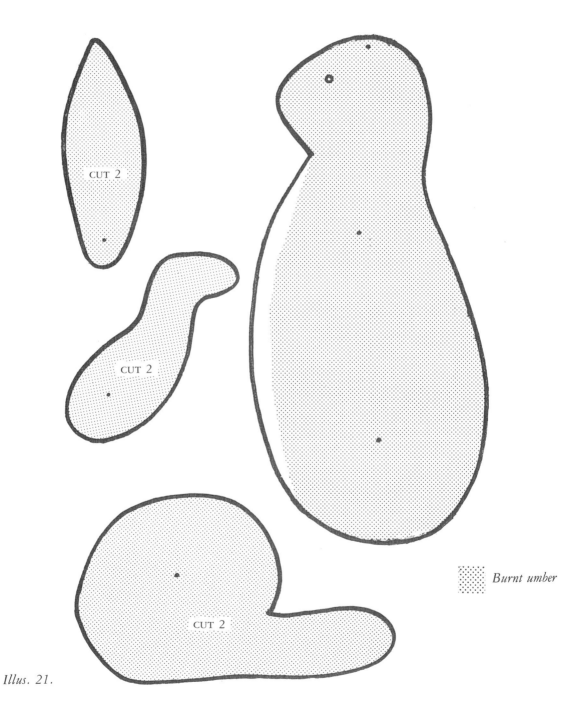

CUT 2

CUT 2

CUT 2

Burnt umber

Illus. 21.

CUT 2

CUT 2

CUT 2

TOOLS

Scroll saw or band saw
Drill with ⅛-in. bit (⁷⁄₆₄-in. bit if dowels are thinner)
Stationary belt sander or sanding wheel (optional): with medium-grade sandpaper
Small hammer
Wood nippers

INSTRUCTIONS

Pattern. Trace pattern pieces onto paper, marking holes to be drilled. Cut out. Then trace around pattern onto heavy paper or poster board and cut out.

Lay poster-board pattern for rabbit's body onto ¾-in. wood, making sure the pattern runs lengthwise with the grain of the wood (Illus. 22). Trace. Then trace pattern for two forelegs and two hind legs onto the ⅜-in. wood, also keeping the grain lengthwise. Trace pattern for two ears onto ¼-in. wood.

Cutting. With scroll or band saw, cut out body, legs, and ears.

Drilling. Drill holes in pieces as marked. Be sure to drill as straight as possible so that the rabbit will stand straight. A drill press or drill stand will simplify this step.

Sanding. Sanding gives the rabbits their personality, depending on how much and where you sand. Starting with the body, move the edges against the sander (Illus. 4) or sand by hand with medium-grade sandpaper at right angles to produce a rounded, carved effect. Sand the legs in the same manner that you sanded the body, but on the inside where they join the body, sand surface and edges lightly, retaining square edges. Sand the ears for a rounded effect. Going with the grain, give each piece a final sanding by hand with a fine-grade sandpaper.

Painting. *Cocoa Bunny:* First, draw lines on both sides where light-colored tummy should end. Next, mix ¼ tsp. of titanium white paint with a tiny drop of burnt umber. This should mix to a pale beige. Paint tummy area.

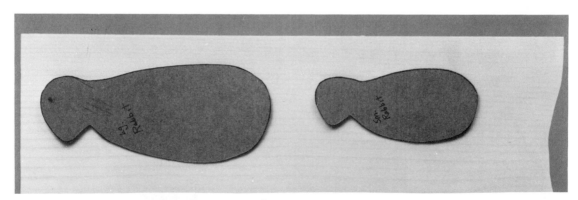

Illus. 22. Laying the poster-board pattern on the wood: be sure the pattern runs lengthwise with the grain of the wood.

Combine about ½ tsp. each of burnt umber and titanium white, using slightly more burnt umber. Mix well. Paint remainder of body, then the legs and ears.

Whenever paint dries out on brush, dip it into water. Cover unused mixed paint with plastic wrap for later use on touch-ups. Let dry approximately one hour.

Marshmallow: Mix a tiny drop of burnt umber with 1½ tsp. of titanium white to produce an off-white. Paint the entire rabbit this color. Save unused paint. Let dry for approximately one hour.

Assembling. For each rabbit cut four wooden dowels approximately ⅞ in. long and two dowels ¾ in. long. If wood thickness varies from recommended dimensions, alter length of dowels accordingly. Round ends with sandpaper.

Insert dowels by placing two small blocks of wood about ½ to 1 in. apart on work surface (see Illus. 25). Set one rabbit leg on top of blocks (outside facing up) with drilled hole above opening between blocks. Place a ⅞-in. piece of dowel at

drilled hole. Hammer in, leaving 1/16 in. of dowel showing on outside. Repeat procedure with the other legs. Use ¾-in. dowels for ears. Follow same procedure for other rabbit.

Press, or lightly hammer, legs and ears into place, leaving 1/16 in. of dowel extended. Use wood blocks as needed.

Touch up protruding ends of dowels with leftover paint.

If the rabbit does not stand straight, try moving legs so they are flat on the bottom. Also, try squeezing legs in to meet body. If both fail, then the reason why the rabbit tilts is because the dowel holes were not drilled straight. You can remedy this by sanding the uneven bottom of the rabbit at a 90° angle to the sander until flat. Hand sand lightly and use touch-up paint.

Eyes. First paint a small dot of titanium white for the eyes. When dry, paint a smaller dot of black inside the white dot and towards the nose.

Piggy

MATERIALS

Softwood, ¾ in. thick: one piece
2½ x 4 in.
Softwood, ⅜ in. thick: one piece 2 x 4 in.
Birch plywood, ¼ in. thick: one piece
1½ x 2 in.
Wooden dowel: ⅛ in. diameter,
4 in. long
Acrylic paint: titanium white, burnt
umber, naphthol red light, black, and permanent green deep
Permanent waterproof marker with fine
point: black
Sandpaper: medium and fine grades
Brushes: ¾ in. bright and 1/16 in. round
Wood glue

TOOLS

Scroll saw or band saw
Drill with ⅛-in. bit (7/64-in. bit if dowels
are thinner)
Stationary belt sander or sanding wheel
(optional): with medium-grade sandpaper
Small hammer
Wood nippers

INSTRUCTIONS

Pattern. Trace all pattern pieces for the
pig onto paper, marking holes to be
drilled, and cut out. Then transfer patterns to heavy paper or poster board and
cut out.

Lay the poster-board pattern of the pig's
body onto ¾-in. wood. Be sure it runs
lengthwise with the grain of the wood

Illus. 23.

(Illus. 22). Trace. Then trace pattern for two forelegs and two hind legs onto the ⅜-in. wood. Trace two ears and one watermelon slice onto ¼-in. birch plywood.

Cutting. With the scroll or band saw, cut out the pig's body, legs, ears, and the watermelon, being very careful not to cut your fingers when working on the small pieces.

Drilling. Drill holes in pieces where marked, using drill stand if available. Straight holes are necessary so the pig will sit level.

Sanding. This step is just as critical as the drilling. Sanding gives the toys their personality. Starting with the pig's body, move the edges against the sander at right angles to produce a rounded, carved effect (Illus. 4). Or sand by hand with the grain of the wood using medium-grade sandpaper.

Sand the legs as you did the body, being especially careful of your fingers. Sand the ears and watermelon by hand. Give each piece a final sanding by hand with a fine-grade sandpaper, going with the grain.

Prior to painting, glue the pig's ears in place, using only a drop or two of glue. Let dry.

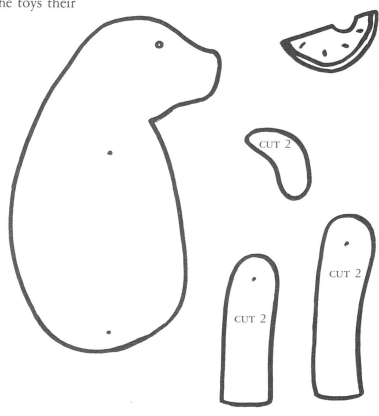

Illus. 24.

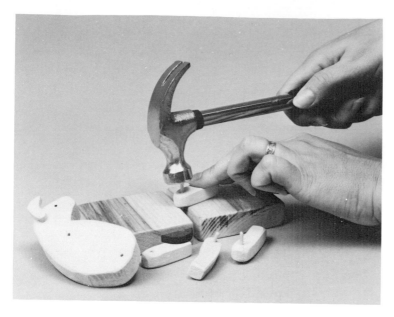

Illus. 25. Inserting dowels: place two small blocks of wood on work surface, set one of the legs on top of the blocks, and hammer in dowel as shown.

Painting. Mix ¾ tsp. of titanium white with a tiny drop of burnt umber and a tiny drop of naphthol red light to produce a pale, beige pink. Paint the entire pig this color. Let dry. Cover and save any unused paint for touch-ups.

Next, mix ⅛ tsp. of naphthol red light with a tiny drop of black to produce a dark red. Paint the top and sides of the watermelon slice. Let dry. Mix ⅛ tsp. of permanent green deep with a pinpoint drop of black to produce a darker shade of green. Paint the bottom and about ¹⁄₁₆ in. of the side edges of the watermelon. Let dry.

Assembling. Cut four wooden dowels ⅛-in. diameter and approximately ⅞ in. long. Round ends with sandpaper. Insert dowels by placing two small blocks of wood ½ to 1 in. apart on work surface (see Illus. 25). Put one leg on top of

blocks with drilled hole above opening between blocks. Place a piece of dowel above drill hole and hammer in, leaving ¹⁄₁₆ in. of dowel showing on outside. Repeat procedure with remaining legs. Press, or lightly hammer, legs into body, leaving the ¹⁄₁₆-in. piece of dowel extended. Use wood blocks as needed. Touch-up protruding ends of dowels with leftover paint.

Watermelon. Draw four seeds with a pointed, black, waterproof marker. Place a drop or two of glue on the back of the watermelon and position watermelon in the pig's left foreleg, holding it there for a moment or two while the glue dries.

Eyes. First, paint a small dot of titanium white for the eye. When dry, paint a smaller dot of black inside the white dot and towards the nose.

Bitsybear, American Bear, and Honeybear

MATERIALS
Bitsybear
Softwood, ¾ in. thick: one piece
3 x 4 in.
Softwood, ⅜ in. thick: one piece
3 x 5½ in.
Birch plywood, ¼ in. thick: one piece
2 x 2 in.

Honeybear or American Bear
Softwood, ¾ in. thick: one piece
4½ x 7½ in.
Softwood, ⅜ in. thick: one piece 5 x 9 in.
Birch plywood, ¼ in. thick: one piece
3 x 3½ in.
Permanent waterproof markers with fine
points (American Bear only): red and
blue

All bears
Wooden dowel: ⅛ in. diameter, 15 in.
long
Acrylic paint: burnt umber, naphthol red
light, titanium white, and black
Sandpaper: medium and fine grades
Brushes: ¾ in. bright and 1/16 in. round
Wood glue

TOOLS
Scroll saw or band saw
Drill with ⅛-in. bit (7/64-in. bit if dowels
are thinner)
Stationary belt sander or sanding wheel
(optional): with medium-grade sandpaper
Small hammer
Wood nippers

Illus. 26.

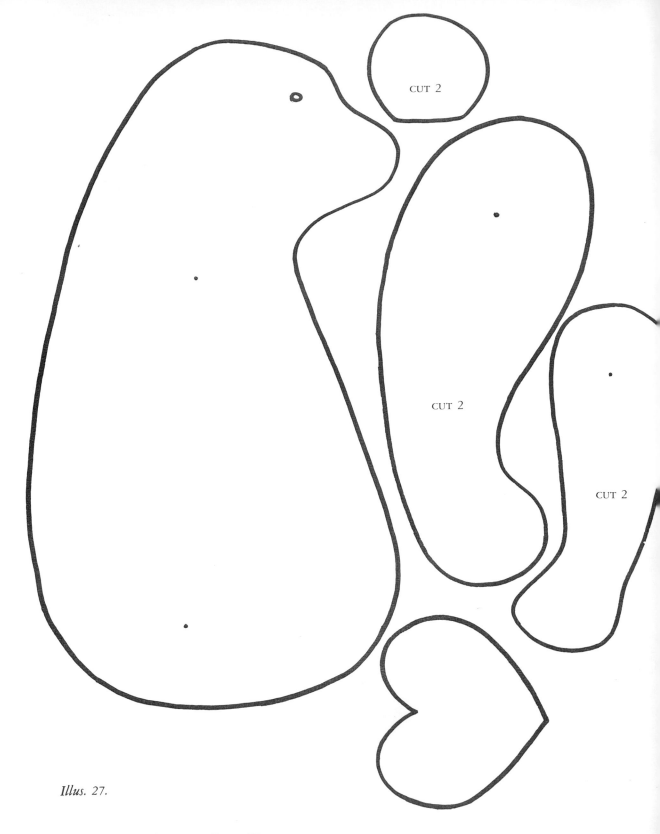

CUT 2

CUT 2

CUT 2

Illus. 27.

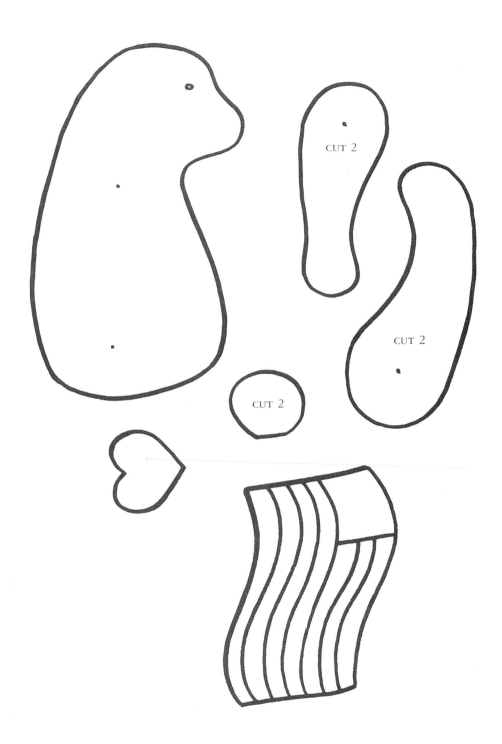

CUT 2

CUT 2

CUT 2

INSTRUCTIONS

Pattern. Trace all pattern pieces for bear onto paper, marking holes to be drilled, and cut out. Then trace around pattern onto heavy paper or poster board and cut these out. Lay poster-board pattern for the bear's body onto ¾-in. wood, making sure the pattern runs lengthwise with the grain of the wood (Illus. 22). Trace.

Next, trace the poster-board pattern for the legs onto the ⅜-in. wood. Trace poster-board pattern for the ears, heart, and flag onto the ¼-in. wood.

Cutting. With scroll or band saw, cut out the body, legs, and heart or flag.

Drilling. Drill holes in pieces as marked. Be sure to drill as straight as possible, using a drill stand, if available.

Using the same bit, drill a ¾-in. hole into the bottom of the flag for the pole. Also drill a hole in American Bear's right paw, from top to bottom.

Sanding. Sanding gives the bears their personality, depending on how and where you sand.

Starting with the body, move the edges against the sander at right angles to produce a rounded, carved effect (Illus. 4). Or sand by hand with the grain of the wood using medium-grade sandpaper. Sand the forelegs and hind legs in the same way as you did the body, but on the inside surfaces where they meet the body

sand only lightly, retaining the squared edges.

Sand ears and heart, or flag, by hand. Going with the grain, give each piece a final sanding by hand with a fine-grade sandpaper.

Before painting, attach the ears to the bear's body with a drop or two of glue. Let dry.

Painting. For each bear mix ¾ tsp. each of burnt umber and naphthol red light to produce a rust color. Paint body and legs of bear. Let dry approximately one hour. Cover and save any unused paint for touch-ups.

Mix ¼ tsp. of naphthol red light with a pinpoint drop of black. This should produce dark red. Paint heart.

Assembling. For each bear cut four wooden dowels, approximately ⅞ in. long. Round ends with sandpaper. Cut a 3-in. dowel for flag.

Insert dowels by placing two small blocks of wood about ½ to 1 in. apart on work surface (see Illus. 25). Put one of the legs on top of blocks (outside facing up) with drilled hole above the opening between the blocks. Place a piece of dowel above hole and hammer in, leaving ⅟₁₆ in. of dowel showing on the outside. Repeat for remaining legs.

Press or lightly hammer legs into body,

leaving the 1/16-in. piece of dowel extended. Touch up protruding ends of dowels with leftover paint. Save the 3-in. dowel for the flag.

Heart. Place a drop or two of glue on the back of the heart and place in the bear's right paw. Hold it in place for a moment or two to let the glue dry.

Flag. Draw light pencil lines on both sides of the flag as indicated. Using permanent ink markers, paint every other stripe red. Leave remaining stripes natural.

Use blue marker for the square. This may also be done in acrylics if you paint well.

Eyes. Paint a small dot of titanium white for the eyes. When dry, paint a smaller dot of black inside the white dot and towards the nose.

After the flag is dry, insert the 3-in. dowel into the drilled hole and push it into the bear's paw. You may need to sand the top and bottom ½ in. of the dowel rather well, so that it will fit easily.

Mama Duck & Duckling

MATERIALS
Mama Duck
Softwood, ¾ in. thick: one piece
8½ x 12 in.
Softwood, ⅜ in. thick: one piece
7½ x 8 in.

Duckling
Softwood, ¾ in. thick: one piece 4 x 5 in.
Softwood, ⅜ in. thick: one piece 3 x 6 in.

Both Ducks
Wooden dowel: ⅛ in. diameter, 4 in. long
Acrylic paint: titanium white, burnt umber, naphthol red light, black, and cadmium yellow medium

Sandpaper: medium and fine grades
Brushes: ¾ in. bright and ¹⁄₁₆ in. round

TOOLS
Scroll saw or band saw
Drill with ⅛-in. bit (⁷⁄₆₄-in. bit if dowels are thinner)
Stationary belt sander or sanding wheel (optional): with medium-grade sandpaper
Small hammer
Wood nippers

INSTRUCTIONS
Pattern. Trace pattern pieces onto paper, marking holes to be drilled, and cut out. Then trace around pattern onto heavy paper or poster board and cut out.

Lay the poster-board pattern for both Mama Duck and Duckling onto ¾-in.

Illus. 28.

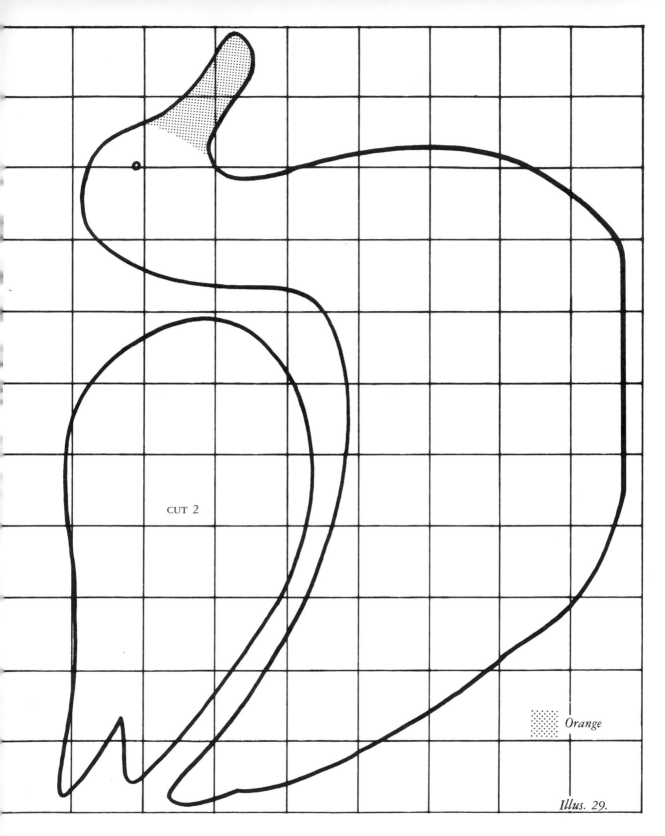

CUT 2

Orange

Illus. 29.

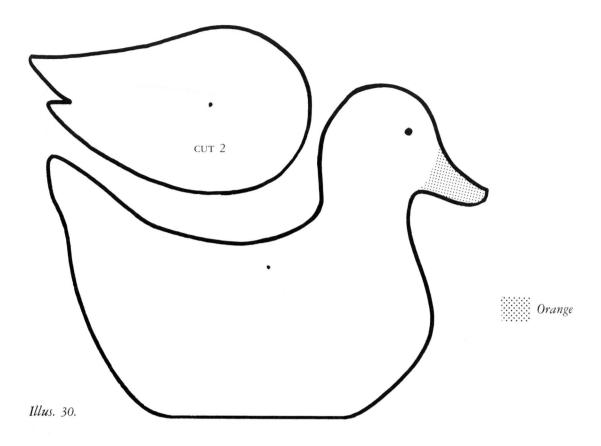

CUT 2

Orange

Illus. 30.

wood. Trace. Onto ⅜-in. wood, trace poster-board pattern for two wings for each duck. Make sure the patterns run lengthwise with the grain of the wood (Illus. 22).

Cutting. Using the scroll or band saw, cut out the duck bodies and wings. Be sure to use relief cuts for very curved areas (see Illus. 3).

Drilling. Drill holes in body and wings where marked, using a drill stand if possible to ensure straight penetration.

Sanding. Sanding is extremely important

because it gives the toys their personality, depending on how much and where you sand.

Starting with the body, move the edges against the sander at right angles to produce a rounded, carved effect (Illus. 4). Or sand by hand with the grain of the wood, using a medium-grade sandpaper.

Sand the wings in the same way, but sand the inside edge only slightly. The outside edge should be sanded to produce the carved look. Give each piece a final sanding by hand with a fine-grade sandpaper, going with the grain.

Painting. Draw paint lines for the beak. Next, mix a small drop of burnt umber with 3 tsp. of titanium white to tone down the stark whiteness. Paint body and wings and let dry.

Mix ¼ tsp. of cadmium yellow medium with a few drops of naphthol red light and a drop of burnt umber to produce a "beak" orange. Paint the beaks and let dry. Cover unused white paint for later touch-ups.

Assembling. Using nippers, cut four lengths of wooden dowels approximately ⅞ in. long. Round the ends with sandpaper.

Insert dowels by placing two small blocks of wood about ½ to 1 in. apart on work surface (see Illus. 25). Set a wing on top of the blocks (outside facing up) with the drilled hole above opening between blocks. Lightly hammer in one of the cut pieces of dowel, leaving 1⁄16 in. of dowel showing on the outside. Repeat procedure for the other wings.

Press or lightly hammer in the wings, leaving the 1⁄16 in. of dowel showing. Touch-up the protruding ends of the dowels with leftover paint.

Eyes. Paint a small drop of titanium white for the eyes. When dry, paint a smaller black dot inside the white dot and towards the beak.

Pan & Nandy Pandas

MATERIALS
Pan
Softwood, ¾ in. thick: one piece
4½ x 7½ in.
Softwood, ⅜ in. thick: one piece
5 x 9 in.

Nandy
Softwood, ¾ in. thick: one piece 3 x 4 in.
Softwood, ⅜ in. thick: one piece
3 x 5½ in.

Both Pandas
Birch plywood for ears, ¼ in. thick: one
piece 3 x 3 in.
Wooden dowel: ⅛ in. diameter, 8 in. long
Acrylic paint: titanium white, mars black,
and burnt umber
Sandpaper: medium and fine grades
Brushes: ¾ in. bright and ¹⁄₁₆ in. round
Wood glue

TOOLS
Scroll saw or band saw
Drill with ⅛-in. bit (⁷⁄₆₄-in. bit if dowels
are thinner)

Illus. 31.

Stationary belt sander or sanding wheel (optional): with medium-grade sandpaper
Small hammer
Wood nippers

INSTRUCTIONS

Pattern. Trace pattern pieces onto paper, marking holes to be drilled, and cut out. Then trace around pattern onto heavy paper or poster board and cut out.

Lay poster-board pattern for panda's body onto ¾-in. wood, making sure pattern is lengthwise with the grain of the wood (Illus. 22). Trace. Onto ⅜-in. wood, trace pattern for forelegs and hind legs, also keeping grain lengthwise. Trace pattern for two ears onto ¼-in. wood.

Cutting. Using scroll saw or band saw, cut out body, legs, and ears.

Drilling. Drill holes in pieces where marked. Be sure to drill straight using a drill press or drill stand if available, since this will affect how level the panda will stand.

Sanding. Starting with the body, move the edges against the sander at right angles to produce a rounded, carved effect (Illus. 4). If sanding by hand, use medium-grade sandpaper and rub with the grain of the wood.

Sand the legs in the same manner that you did the body, but on inside surfaces where they meet body sand only lightly, retaining square edges. The other side should be sanded to look carved. Sand the

ears by hand and then give each piece a final hand sanding with fine-grade sandpaper, going with the grain of the wood.

Painting. Draw paint lines on the pandas' bodies (Illus. 32). Mix a tiny drop of burnt umber with 1½ tsp. of titanium white to tone down the whiteness. Paint the white areas. When dry, paint the black areas. Let dry approximately one hour. Cover and save unused paint for touch-ups later.

Assembling. Using nippers, cut four, ⅛-in. wooden dowels, approximately ⅞ in. long for each panda. Round ends with sandpaper.

Insert dowels by placing two small blocks of wood about ½ to 1 in. apart on work surface (see Illus. 25). Set one of the legs on top of blocks (outside facing up) with drilled hole above the opening between the blocks. Lightly hammer in a piece of dowel, leaving 1/16 in. of dowel showing on the outside. Repeat for remaining legs. Press or lightly hammer all legs into panda's body, leaving 1/16 in. of dowel showing. Touch up protruding ends of dowels with leftover paint.

Ears. Attach ears to head with a drop or two of glue.

Eyes. Paint a small dot of titanium white for the eyes. When dry, paint a smaller dot of black inside the white dot and towards the nose.

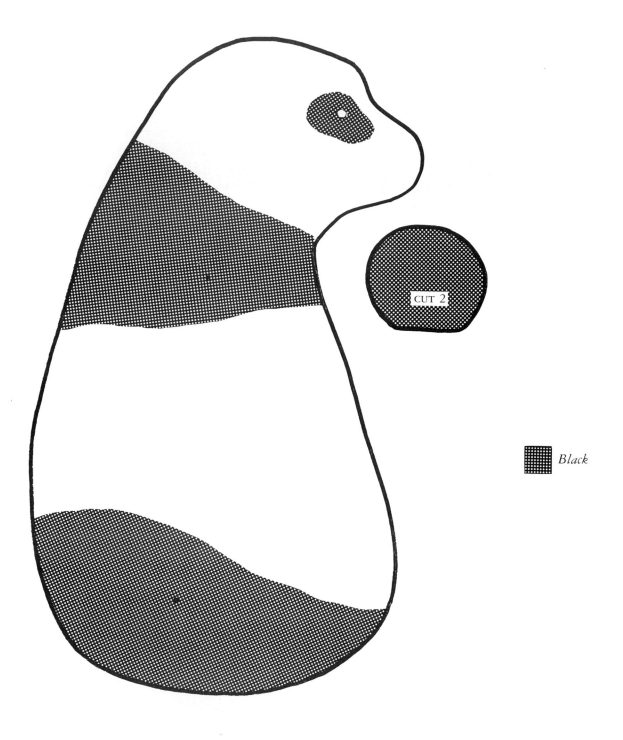

CUT 2

Black

Illus. 32.

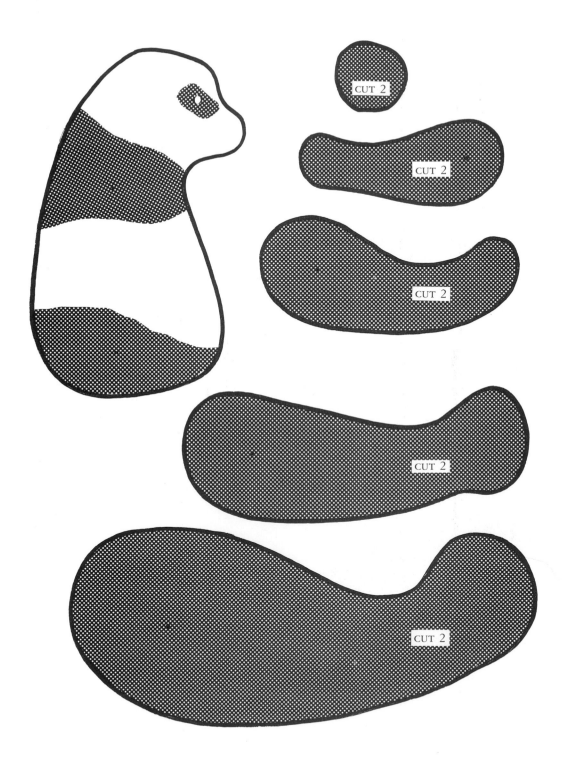

CUT 2

CUT 2

CUT 2

CUT 2

CUT 2

Barney the Cat

MATERIALS

Softwood, ¾ in. thick: one piece
4 x 6½ in.
Softwood, ⅜ in. thick: one piece
5½ x 8 in.
Birch plywood, ¼ in. thick: one piece
1 x 2 in.
Wooden dowels: ⅛ in. diameter, 4 in.
long
Flathead wood screw: ¾ x 4, one
Acrylic paint: titanium white, burnt umber, cadmium yellow medium, naphthol red light, and black
Sandpaper: medium and fine grades
Brushes: ¾ in. bright and ⅟₁₆ in. round
Wood glue

TOOLS

Scroll saw or band saw
Drill with ⅛-in. bit (⅞₄-in. bit if dowels are thinner)
Stationary belt sander or sanding wheel (optional): with medium-grade sandpaper
Small hammer
Wood nippers

Illus. 33.

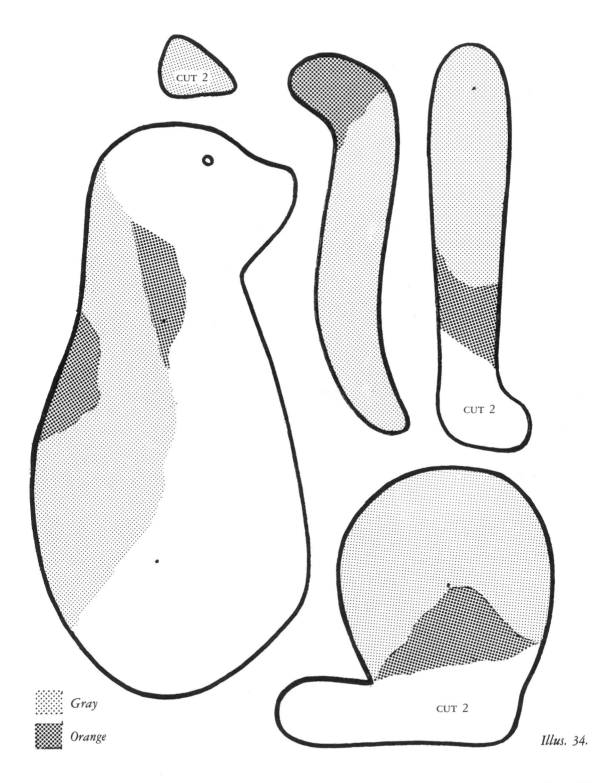

CUT 2

CUT 2

CUT 2

Gray

Orange

Illus. 34.

INSTRUCTIONS

Pattern. Trace pattern pieces onto paper, marking holes to be drilled, and cut out. Then trace around pattern onto heavy paper or poster board and cut out.

Lay poster-board pattern for cat's body onto ¾-in. wood, making sure the pattern lays lengthwise with the grain of the wood (Illus. 22), and trace. Trace poster-board pattern for tail, two forelegs, and two hind legs onto the ⅜-in. wood, also keeping the grain of the wood lengthwise to ensure strength. Finally, trace two ears onto the birch plywood.

Cutting. With scroll or band saw, cut out the cat's body, legs, ears, and tail.

Drilling. Drill holes in pieces where marked. Be sure to drill straight, using a drill stand or drill press, if possible, to ensure straight holes.

Sanding. Starting with the body, move the edges against the sander at right angles to produce a rounded, carved effect (Illus. 4). If sanding by hand use medium-grade sandpaper.

Sand all legs and tail the same way that you did the body, but on inside surfaces where they will meet the body sand only lightly, retaining square edges. Sand the ears by hand and then give all pieces a final hand sanding with a fine-grade sandpaper, going with the grain.

Painting. Draw paint lines on Barney's body, legs, and tail (see Illus. 34). Mix a tiny drop or two of burnt umber with ½ tsp. of titanium white to produce an off-white. Paint all of the white areas.

Next, mix ¼ tsp. of cadmium yellow medium with a tiny drop of naphthol red light and a tiny drop of burnt umber. This should produce a rusty orange color. Paint the rust-colored areas. Now, mix ½ tsp. each of black and white to get gray. Paint remaining areas. Let all pieces dry. Save any unused paint.

Assembling. Using nippers, cut four, ⅛-in. wooden dowels, approximately ⅞ in. long for each panda. Round ends with sandpaper.

Insert dowels by placing two small blocks of wood ½ to 1 in. apart on work surface (see Illus. 25). Set a leg on top of blocks (outside facing up) with drilled hole above opening between blocks. Place a dowel above the hole and lightly hammer in, leaving ¹⁄₁₆ in. of dowel protruding on the outside. Repeat for remaining legs. Press or lightly hammer the legs into cat's body, leaving the ¹⁄₁₆ in. of dowel showing. Touch up protruding ends of dowels with leftover paint.

With a few drops of glue, attach Barney's tail and ears. Let dry. For added strength: drill hole with ⅛-in. bit through tail and into the cat's body; insert and countersink screw.

Eyes. Paint a small dot of titanium white for each eye. When dry, paint a smaller black dot inside the white dot and towards the nose.

See Illus. 33 for correct sitting position for Barney: his forelegs are just in front of his hind legs.

Bosco the Dog

MATERIALS

Softwood, ¾ in. thick: one piece 3 x 6 in.
Softwood, ⅜ in. thick: one piece 5 x 6 in.
Birch plywood, ¼ in. thick: one piece,
1½ x 2 in.
Wooden dowel: ⅛ in. diameter, 4 in.
long
Flathead wood screw: ¾ x 4, one
Acrylic paint: titanium white, burnt
umber, black

Sandpaper: medium and fine grades
Brushes: ¾ in. bright and ¹⁄₁₆ in. round
Wood glue

TOOLS

Scroll saw or band saw
Drill with ⅛-in. bit (⁷⁄₆₄-in. if dowels are
on thin side)
Stationary belt sander or sanding wheel
(optional): with medium-grade sandpaper
Small hammer
Wood nippers

Illus. 35.

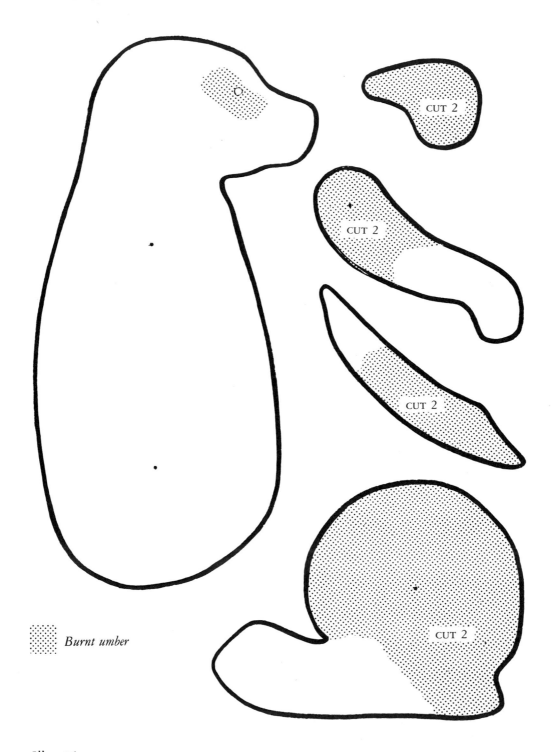

CUT 2

CUT 2

CUT 2

CUT 2

Burnt umber

Illus. 36.

INSTRUCTIONS

Pattern. Trace all pattern pieces onto paper, marking holes to be drilled and cut out. Then trace around the patterns onto heavy paper or poster board and cut out.

Lay poster-board pattern for the dog's body onto ¾-in. wood and trace. Onto ⅜-in. wood, trace the patterns for two forelegs, two hind legs, and tail. Trace two ears onto the birch plywood. In all cases, be sure to lay the patterns lengthwise with the grain of the wood (Illus. 22).

Cutting. Using the scroll or band saw, cut out all pieces for the dog. Be careful of your fingers when cutting out the ears.

Drilling. Drill holes in pieces where marked, using a drill stand or drill press if possible, to ensure straight holes.

Sanding. Starting with the body, move the edges against the sander at right angles to produce a rounded, carved look (Illus. 4). If sanding by hand, use medium-grade sandpaper and rub with the grain.

Sand the legs and tail in the same way that you did the body, but on the inside surfaces where they will meet the body sand only lightly, retaining square edges. Be sure to sand both left and right legs.

Sand the ears by hand. Give all pieces a final hand sanding with fine-grade sandpaper, going with the grain.

Painting. Draw paint lines on Bosco's body and legs (see Illus. 36). Mix 1 tsp. titanium white with a few drops of burnt umber to produce an off-white. Paint white areas. Paint remaining areas burnt umber. Cover and save unused paint.

Assembling. Using nippers, cut four, ⅛-in. wood dowels, approximately ⅞ in. long. Round ends with sandpaper.

To facilitate dowel insertion place two small blocks of wood ½ to 1 in. apart on work surface (see Illus. 25). Set one of the legs on top of blocks (outside facing up) with drilled hole above the opening between the blocks. Place a dowel above the hole and lightly hammer in, leaving ¹⁄₁₆ in. of dowel showing on the outside. Repeat for remaining legs. Now, press or lightly hammer all legs into body, leaving ¹⁄₁₆ in. of dowel showing. Touch up protruding ends of dowels with leftover paint.

With a few drops of glue, attach Bosco's ears and tail. Let dry. For added strength: drill hole with ⅛-in. bit through tail and into the dog's body; insert and countersink screw.

Eyes. Paint a small white dot for each eye. When dry, paint a smaller black dot inside the white dot and towards the nose.

Weather Vanes

WEATHER VANES

eather vanes, also called wind vanes or weathercocks, are devices that turn freely on a vertical rod and point into the wind. One of the most famous, by the 18th-century master vane maker Shem Drowne, is the grasshopper atop Faneuil Hall in Boston, Massachusetts.

These seemingly insignificant examples of folk art have throughout history, however, reflected the rich culture of their makers. Triton, Greek god of the sea, inspired the earliest recorded weather vane. Cast in bronze, this life-size figure, with the head and body of a man and the tail of a fish, pointed his wand in the direction of the wind. He was placed above the Tower of the Winds, built by Andronicus in Athens during the first century B.C.

A popular European motif was the rooster. It originated over 1,000 years ago when all churches were instructed by papal edict to mount a rooster form on their steeples as a reminder to the congregation not to deny their faith as the apostle Peter did when the cock crowed three times. By the 13th century these stationary roosters were made into mobile weathercocks. Early American settlers brought this traditional vane with them, adorning many New England churches. Other designs included fish, sea gulls, and even ships, which bedecked roof tops in coastal towns. Paul Revere placed a wooden codfish studded with copper nails for scales above his silversmith shop in Boston.

But farmers, obviously, could not see the town's vanes, and so they erected their own. And far from the local blacksmith they invented their own designs. Breaking with tradition, the farmers created vanes in the shape of Indians, arrows, and wild and domesticated animals, especially horses. After the Revolution, eagles too became popular.

Beginning in 1875 vanes were mass-produced in metal, using wooden, hand-carved models. Manufacturers advertised hundreds of shapes in elaborate catalogues that reflected the growth of the United States: the railroad, fire-fighting equipment, and farm specialization. But it is the weather vane that represents a simpler way of life, a life closely tied to Nature, that is shown here.

Running Horse Weather Vane

MATERIALS

Birch plywood, ¼ in. thick, or softwood, ⅜ in. thick: one piece 9 x 18 in.
Wood for base: one 2 x 4, 9 in. long
Metal rod, or substitute medium-weight metal clothes hanger: ³⁄₃₂ in. diameter, 8 in. long
Stain for base: reddish-brown tone
Acrylic paint: burnt umber, titanium white, naphthol red light

Brushes: ½ in. flat and ¾ in. bright
Sandpaper: medium and fine grades

TOOLS

Scroll saw or band saw
Drill with ³⁄₃₂-in. bit
Small hammer
Metal cutters

INSTRUCTIONS

Pattern. Trace pattern, including lines for the mane and tail, onto paper, and cut out. Then trace around pattern onto heavy paper or poster board and cut out. Lay poster-board pattern of horse onto

Illus. 37.

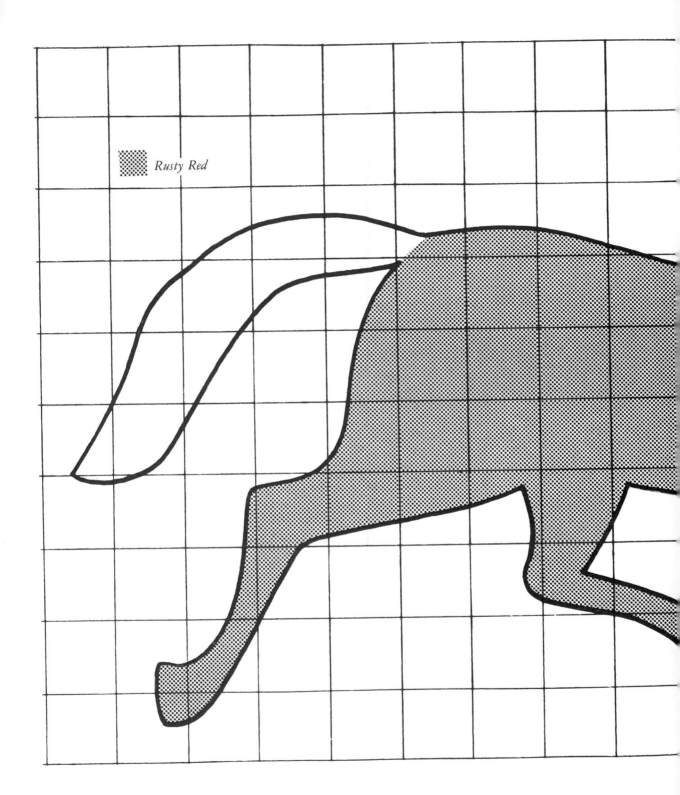

Rusty Red

Illus. 38

9 x 18-in. wood so that the horse is running with the grain of the wood (see Illus. 22). Trace pattern.

Cutting. With scroll or band saw, cut out horse one section at a time. Where two lines meet, forming a **V** (where lines for ears and legs meet, for instance), cut along one line, back out, and then cut along the other line.

Drilling. This hole must be drilled without the help of a drill stand. Draw a line on the side of the horse from the spot to be drilled; this will serve as a guide (see Illus. 38). It is also helpful to position fingers on both sides of the horse (see Illus. 47), drilling slowly so you can feel if the bit is entering the wood straight. Extend the drill bit as far forward as possible, as this is a small space to drill in. Drill hole into the underside of the horse, where marked, to a depth of about ¾ in.

Next, drill a hole into the center of the top side of the 2 x 4-in. base. (Find center by drawing an **X** from corner to corner. Where the lines intersect is the center.)

Sanding. With a small square of medium sandpaper, smooth all edges of the weather vane. Also sand the sides well for a smooth painting surface. Finish by sanding the entire horse with fine sandpaper.

Sand base with medium sandpaper so that the edges are slightly rounded.

Painting. Before painting, outline the mane and tail in pencil. Mix paint for these areas first: a ¼ tsp. of titanium white and a tiny drop of burnt umber. The desired color is a pale beige.

Paint edges, then sides, of mane and tail, using the ½-in. flat-edge brush.

Next, mix 1 tsp. naphthol red light with ¾ tsp. burnt umber. Adjust amounts as necessary to produce a rusty red. Paint remaining edges and then the body, using the ¾-in. brush. Let dry.

Staining. Wearing rubber gloves, dip a small rag into the stain and wipe over all sides of the 2 x 4-in. base. Wipe off excess with a dry cloth. Let dry according to the manufacturer's directions.

Assembling. Cut metal rod 8 in. long. Sand sharp edges. Paint rod with burnt umber and let dry. With a hammer, tap rod into base, then put the running horse on top of the rod and tap lightly into place. If the horse leans in one direction, bend the rod slightly, being careful not to split the wood where the rod is inserted.

Sea Serpent Weather Vane

MATERIALS
Birch plywood, ¼ in. thick, or softwood, ⅜ in. thick: one piece 9 x 13 in.
Wood for base: one 2 x 4, 8½ in. long
Metal rod, or substitute medium-weight metal clothes hanger ³⁄₃₂ in. diameter, 7 in. long
Stain for base: reddish-brown tone

Acrylic paint: chromium oxide green, naphthol red light, burnt umber, black, and white
Brushes: ½ in. flat, ¾ in. bright, ¹⁄₁₆ in. round
Sandpaper: medium and fine grades

TOOLS
Scroll saw or band saw
Drill with ³⁄₃₂-in. and ¼-in. bits
Small hammer
Metal cutters

Illus. 39.

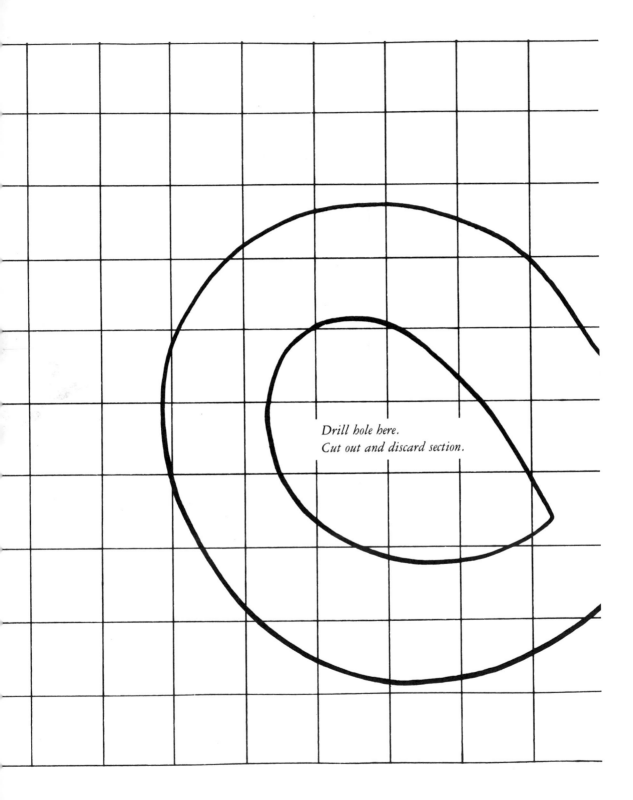

Drill hole here.
Cut out and discard section.

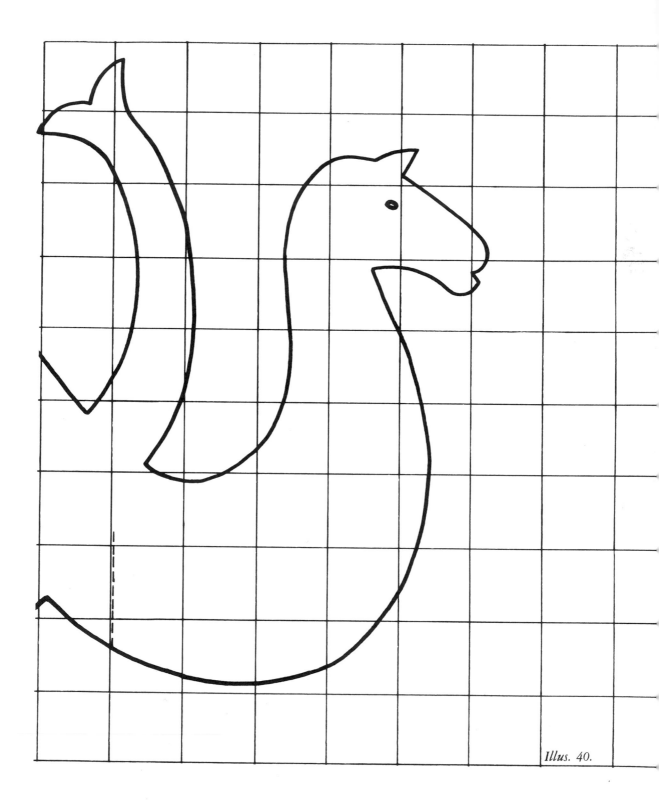

Illus. 40.

INSTRUCTIONS

Pattern. Trace pattern onto paper and cut out. Then trace around pattern onto heavy paper or poster board and cut out. Lay the poster-board pattern of the serpent on the wood so that the pattern is running lengthwise with the grain of the wood (Illus. 22). Trace pattern.

Cutting. With scroll or band saw, cut out the serpent. With a ¼-in., or larger, bit, drill a hole into the center of the tail area to be cut out. This part must be cut out with the scroll saw or a keyhole saw. If using the scroll saw, remove the blade from the saw, insert blade through the drilled hole, and reinsert it into saw. Cut along the inside line of the tail. Now remove the blade from the saw once again, freeing the serpent, and replace the blade. If you don't have a scroll saw, use the keyhole saw. Insert saw into drilled hole and cut along the inside line of the tail.

Drilling. This hole must be drilled without the help of a drill stand. Draw a line in pencil on the side of the serpent from the spot to be drilled (see dotted line in Illus. 40); this will serve as a guide. Hold the serpent on both sides of the area to be drilled, drilling slowly so you can feel if the bit is entering the wood straight (Illus. 47). Drill hole about ¾ in. deep. Next, drill a hole into the center of the top side of the 2 x 4-in. base. Find the center by drawing an **X** from corner to corner. Where the lines intersect is the center.

Sanding. Using medium-grade sandpaper, sand all edges of the serpent. Next, sand the sides smooth. Finish by sanding the entire sea serpent with fine sandpaper.

Sand the edges of base with medium sandpaper so that they are slightly rounded.

Painting. Using the ¾-in. brush, paint the edges and then the body of the sea serpent chromium oxide green. Let dry. With the ½-in. flat-edge brush, paint a ⅛-in. border of naphthol red light around the outside and inside edge. Also, continue the line for the tail so that it crosses in front of the body. Paint red dots on the stomach of the serpent. Let dry. Paint a small white dot for the eye. When dry, paint a smaller black dot inside the white dot and towards the nose.

Staining. Wearing rubber gloves, dip a small rag into the stain and wipe over all sides of the base. Wipe off excess with a dry cloth. Let dry according to the manufacturer's directions.

Assembling. With metal cutters cut metal rod 7 in. long. Sand the edges. Paint the rod with burnt umber and let dry. With a hammer, tap rod into base, then put the sea serpent on top of the rod and tap lightly into place.

Running Rabbit
Weather Vane

MATERIALS
Birch plywood, ¼ in. thick, or softwood,
⅜ in. thick: one piece 7 x 15 in.
Wood for base: one 2 x 4, 6½ in. long
Metal rod, or substitute medium-weight
metal clothes hanger: 3⁄32 in. diameter,
8½ in. long
Stain for base: reddish-brown tone
Acrylic paint: titanium white, burnt
umber, mars black
Brushes: ¾ in. bright and 1⁄16 in. round
Sandpaper: medium and fine grades

TOOLS
Scroll saw or band saw
Drill with 3⁄32-in. bit
Small hammer
Metal cutters

INSTRUCTIONS
Pattern. Trace pattern onto paper and cut
out. Then trace around pattern onto
heavy paper or poster board and cut out.
Lay poster-board pattern of rabbit on
wood so that the rabbit is running with
the grain of the wood (Illus. 22). Trace
pattern.

Illus. 41.

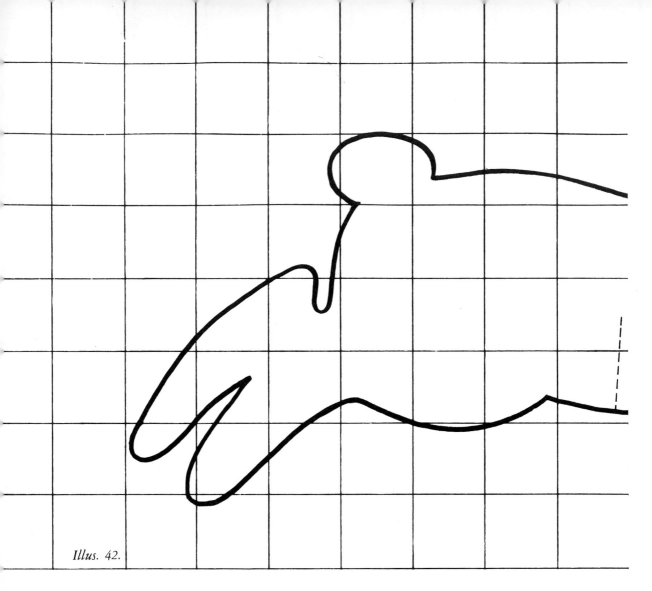

Illus. 42.

Cutting. With scroll or band saw, carefully cut out the rabbit. Where two lines meet—at neck and ears, for instance—cut along one line, back out, and then cut along the other line.

Drilling. Draw a line on the side of the rabbit from the spot to be drilled (see Illus. 42 for dotted line); this will serve as a guide. Hold the rabbit on both sides of the drilling area, drilling slowly so you can feel if the bit is entering the wood straight (Illus. 47). Drill hole about ¾ in. deep.

Next, drill a hole into the center of the top side of the 2 x 4-in. base. Find center by drawing an **X** from corner to corner. Where the lines intersect is the center.

Sanding. Using medium-grade sandpaper, sand all edges of the rabbit. Sand the sides for a smooth surface. Finish by sanding the entire rabbit with fine sandpaper.

Sand edges of base with medium sandpaper so that they are slightly rounded.

Painting. Mix a few drops of burnt umber with a small amount of titanium white to produce an off-white. Paint the entire rabbit, edges first, with the ¾-in. brush. Paint a dot of black for the eye with the ¹⁄₁₆-in. brush. Let dry.

Staining. Wearing rubber gloves, dip a small rag into the stain and wipe over all sides of the base. Wipe off excess with a dry cloth. Let dry according to manufacturer's directions.

Assembling. With metal cutters cut metal rod 8½ in. long. Sand the edges. Paint the rod with burnt umber and let dry. With a hammer, tap rod into base. Then set the rabbit on top of the rod and tap lightly into place.

Goat Weather Vane

MATERIALS

Birch plywood, ¼ in. thick, or softwood,
⅜ in. thick: one piece 9 x 13 in.
Wood for base: one 2 x 4, 5 in. long
Metal rod or substitute medium-weight
metal clothes hanger: ³⁄₃₂ in. diameter,
6 in. long
Stain for base: reddish-brown tone

Acrylic paint: mars black, titanium white,
burnt umber
Brushes: ½ in. flat, ¾ in. bright, ¹⁄₁₆ in.
round
Sandpaper: medium and fine grades

TOOLS

Scroll saw or band saw
Drill with ³⁄₃₂-in. bit
Small hammer
Metal cutters

Illus. 43.

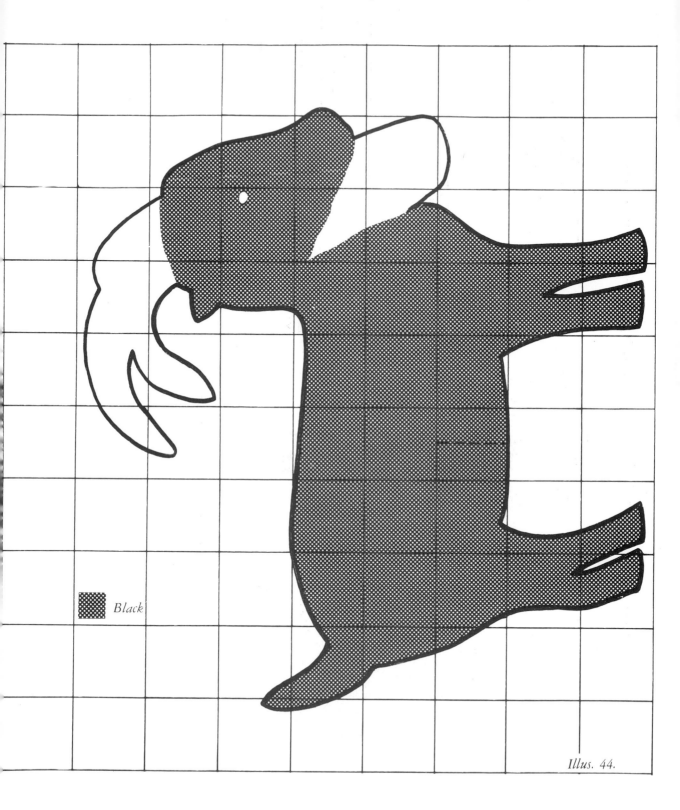

Black

Illus. 44.

INSTRUCTIONS

Pattern. Trace pattern for the goat, including lines for the horns and beard, onto paper and cut out. Then trace around pattern onto heavy paper or poster board and cut out. Lay poster-board pattern of the goat onto the 9 x 13-in. wood with the grain running lengthwise (Illus. 22). Trace pattern.

Cutting. Using the scroll or band saw, cut out the goat. Follow the pattern outline until you reach a **V**-shaped intersection, where legs meet, for instance; stop sawing, back out, and then saw towards the intersection along the other line.

Drilling. First, draw a line on the side of the goat from the spot marked to be drilled (see dotted line in Illus. 44); this will serve as a guide. Also helpful is to position thumbs and fingers on sides of the goat (see Illus. 47), drilling slowly so you can feel if the bit is drilling straight into the wood. Drill the hole to a depth of about ¾ in.

Next, drill a hole into the top side of the 2 x 4-in. base. Find the center by drawing an **X** from corner to corner. Where the lines intersect is the center.

Sanding. With a small square of medium sandpaper, sand edges and sides of the goat. Finish by sanding the entire goat with a fine-grade sandpaper.

Sand edges of base with medium sandpaper so that they are slightly rounded.

Painting. Outline the beard and horns of goat (see Illus. 44). Mix a tiny drop of burnt umber with ¼ tsp. of titanium white to produce an off-white color. Paint beard and horns with the ½-in. brush. Next, paint the remainder of the goat with mars black, using the ¾-in. brush. Let dry. Paint a small dot of white for the eye using ⅟₁₆-in. brush. When dry, paint a smaller black dot inside and to the front of the white dot.

Staining. Wearing rubber gloves, dip a small rag into the stain and wipe over all sides of the 2 x 4-in. base. Wipe off excess with a dry cloth. Let dry according to the manufacturer's directions.

Assembling. Cut metal rod 6 in. long. Sand the edges. Paint the rod with burnt umber and let dry. With a hammer, tap rod into base, then position the goat on top of the rod and tap lightly into place.

Pig Weather Vane

MATERIALS
Birch plywood, ¼-in. thick, or softwood, ⅜ in. thick: one piece 7 x 11 in.
Wood for base: one 2 x 4, 6½ in. long
Metal rod or substitute medium-weight metal clothes hanger: 3/32 in. diameter, 6 in. long
Stain for base: reddish-brown tone
Acrylic paint: burnt umber, titanium white, mars black

Brushes: ¾ in. bright and 1/16 in. round
Sandpaper: medium and fine grades

TOOLS
Scroll saw or band saw
Drill with 3/32-in. bit
Small hammer
Metal cutters

INSTRUCTIONS
Pattern. Trace pattern for pig, including paint lines, onto paper and cut out. Then trace around the pattern onto heavy paper

Illus. 45.

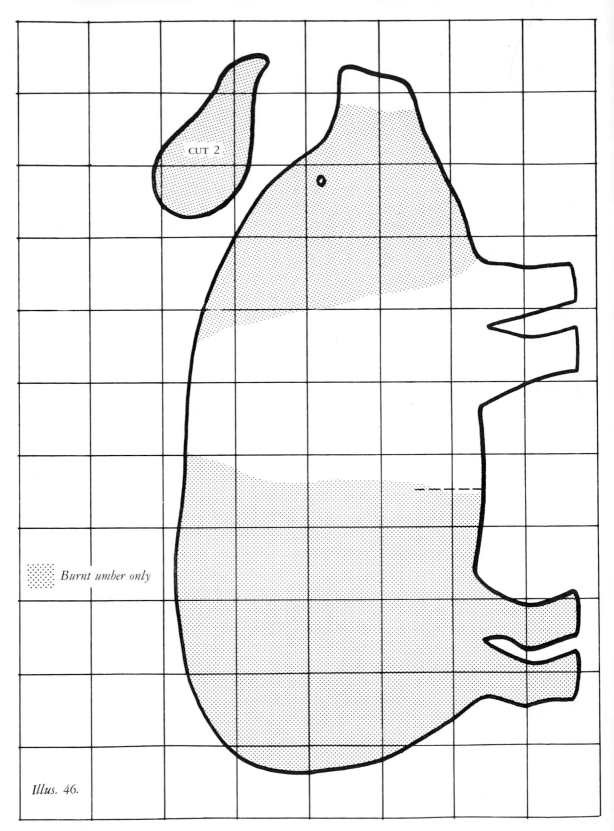

CUT 2

Burnt umber only

Illus. 46.

or poster board and cut out. Lay the poster-board pattern on the wood with the grain running lengthwise (Illus. 22). Trace pattern.

Cutting. With scroll or band saw, cut out pig and pig's ears. When cutting into small spaces, such as between the legs, cut along one line, back out, and then cut along the other.

Drilling. First, draw a line on the side of the pig from the spot marked to be drilled (see dotted line in Illus. 46). This will serve as a guide. Hold pig on both sides of area to be drilled (Illus. 47), drilling slowly so you can feel if the bit is entering the wood straight. Drill the hole about ¾ in. deep. Then drill a hole into the center of the base. Draw an **X** from corner to corner and mark center where lines intersect.

Sanding. With medium-grade sandpaper, sand all edges of the pig. Sand sides and then finish by sanding entire pig with fine sandpaper. Sand the base with medium sandpaper so that the edges are slightly rounded.

Painting. Draw paint lines on pig where indicated in Illus. 46. Paint middle area and nose with titanium white mixed with burnt umber to produce a dark tan color. Next, paint remaining areas with burnt umber. Paint a small white dot for the eye using ⅟₁₆-in. brush. When dry, paint a smaller black dot inside of the white dot and towards the nose.

Staining. Wearing rubber gloves, dip a small rag into the stain and wipe over all sides of the base. Wipe off excess with a dry cloth. Let dry according to manufacturer's directions.

Assembling. Cut a metal rod 6 in. long. Paint the rod with burnt umber and let dry. With a hammer, tap rod into base. Then position the pig on top of the rod and tap lightly into place.

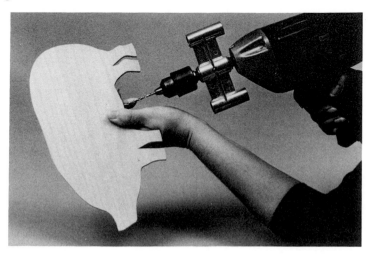

Illus. 47. Drilling: hold the wood on both sides of the area to be drilled so that you can tell if the bit is entering straight.

METRIC CONVERSION CHART

Inches to Millimetres and Centimetres

inches	mm	cm	inches	cm	inches	cm
⅓	3	0.3	9	22.9	30	76.2
¼	6	0.6	10	25.4	31	78.7
⅜	10	1.0	11	27.9	32	81.3
½	13	1.3	12	30.5	33	83.8
⅝	16	1.6	13	33.0	34	86.4
¾	19	1.9	14	35.6	35	88.9
⅞	22	2.2	15	38.1	36	91.4
1	25	2.5	16	40.6	37	94.0
1¼	32	3.2	17	43.2	38	96.5
1½	38	3.8	18	45.7	39	99.1
1¾	44	4.4	19	48.3	40	101.6
2	51	5.1	20	50.8	41	104.1
2½	64	6.4	21	53.3	42	106.7
3	76	7.6	22	55.9	43	109.2
3½	89	8.9	23	58.4	44	111.8
4	102	10.2	24	61.0	45	114.3
4½	114	11.4	25	63.5	46	116.8
5	127	12.7	26	66.0	47	119.4
6	152	15.2	27	68.6	48	121.9
7	178	17.8	28	71.1	49	124.5
8	203	20.3	29	73.7	50	127.0

AMERICAN & BRITISH TERMS

American terms appear on the left; British terms, on the right.

American	British
C-clamp	G cramp
finishing nails	lost head nails
flathead screw	countersink screw
lumber	timber
poster board	card
rubber gloves	thin utility gloves or surgeon's gloves
sandpaper	glasspaper
screw eye	wood screw with ringed shank
tracing paper	transparent paper
unwoven cotton	cotton wool

BIBLIOGRAPHY

Foley, Daniel J. *Toys Through the Ages.* New York: Chilton Books, 1962.

King, Constance Eileen. *The Encyclopedia of Toys.* New York: Crown Publishers, Inc., 1978.

Lipman, Jean and Winchester, Alice. *The Flowering of American Folk Art.* New York: Viking Press, 1974.

White, Gwen. *Antique Toys and Their Background.* New York: Arco Publishing, 1971.

INDEX

Numbers in italics refer to pages with illustrations.

A

Acrylic fibre. *See* Roving
American bear, 59–63

B

Barney the cat, 72–74
Bears, 59–63
Bitsybear, 59–63
Bosco the dog, 75–77
Bunnies, 51–55

C

Cat. *See* Barney the cat
Cocoa bunny, 51–55
Craft fur. *See* Roving

D

Dog. *See* Bosco the dog

Dowels
    for articulated toys, 19
    cutting, for wheels, *37*
    inserting, for articulated toys, *58*
    for wheels, 19
Drilling, correct hand position for, *99*
Duckling, 64–67
Ducks, 64–67

E

Ears, cutting out section to form two, *32*
Enlarging patterns, 11

F

Folk art
    American, 13–14
    decorating with, 13
    designing, 15
    development of, 13
    modern, 13
    motifs, 13

as toys, 13–14
Folk toys
    articulated, 49–77
    designing original patterns for, 15–16, *16*
    development of, 49
    equipment for making, 21–22
    materials for making, 19–21
    rocking horse, 25–32
    wheel toys, 33–48
    wood selection for, 17–18

G

Goat, 94–96
Goat on wheels, 45–48
Grain. *See* Wood

H

Honeybear, 59–63
Horses
    the rocking horse, 25
    rocking horse, 27–32
    running horse weather vane, 83–86

M

Mama duck, 64–67
Marshmallow bunny, 51–55

N

Nandy panda, 68–71

P

Pandas, 68–71
Pan panda, 68–71
Patterns, designing original, 15–16, *16*
Pig, 97–99
Piggy, 56–58
Pony on wheels, 40–44

R

Reindeer on wheels, 35–39
Relief cuts, *21*
Rocking horse, 27–32
    development of, 25
Roving, 20, *20*
Running horse, 83–86
Running rabbit, 91–93

S

Saws
    band, 21
    keyhole, 90
    tabletop scroll, 21
Sander, 21
Sanding, to achieve carved effect, *22*
Sanding wheel, 21–22, *22*
Sea serpent, 87–90

W

Weather vanes, 79–99
    development of, 81
    equipment for making, 21–22

   materials for making, 19–21
   wood selection for, 17–18
Wheel toys, 33–48
   development of, 33
Wood
   glue for, 20
   grain direction and patterns, 54
   selection, 17–18
   sizes, 19

PHOTO CREDIT

Photography by Tamte-Wilson Photography
Norfolk, Virginia

ABOUT THE AUTHOR

Sharon Pierce is a self-taught folk artist. She has been designing toys for her children since they were young. Presently, she designs and makes folk toys and folk art, which she sells to museum gift shops, country shops, and collectors across the country. Photographs of her work have appeared in several publications, including *Country Living* magazine.

An advocate of instructional books, she has also taught herself the crafts of macrame, batik, quilting, and stained glass making.

She lives with her husband and five children in Virginia.